Facebook Foodie
RECIPES OF THE LIKED AND SHARED

Monique Labat

2017-12-06

Happy Foodie Journey!
Best Monique

I dedicate this book to Francesco, my inspirational partner in life's adventures. *Grazie mille Caro* for this wonderful journey we share together.

Cover photography by Craig Scott. Health bread recipe photo by Lisa Coleman.
All other photographs by the author.

Design and layout Jo Petzer of Cosmic Creations
Printed by CreateSpace an Amazon.com company

ISBN 978-0-9946808-0-8

First edition September 2016
First impression September 2016

The reason for compiling this collection of recipes is simple. Back in 2009, I started my Facebook page. It was a fun way of staying in touch with friends and family. Up went photos of special dishes, food experiments and lots of homemade concoctions. Then came Ballymaloe. During the 3-month course I took over 8 000 food and wine related photographs with my Sony Cyber-shot. On Facebook, friends 'liked' and 'shared' the photos and kept asking for the recipes. I trawled back through 3 years of Facebook history and documented which recipes had received the most likes, shares and comments. This collection of recipes comes from my Facebook page, from family and friends, all of which tells a very sentimental story.

Acknowledgments

Thanks to special friends who have sat around our dining-room table and shared their stories, displayed great enthusiasm and enjoyed debating on all matters relating to food and wine, whilst simultaneously demonstrating a healthy appetite!

My thanks to Professor David Walker for his insight into self-publishing. David was generous with his knowledge and advice.

A special thank you to Ali for suggesting the sub-title for the cookbook, to Janine for all the publishing tips and marketing ideas and to Grant for his advice on securing orders!

Contents

Introduction

Tradition is a wonderful thing. It connects you to history, makes for wonderful experiences and allows cherished memories in that special place in your heart. My mother kept every wine label from bottles served at my parents' dinner parties. On the back of each label, Mamie would write down who was at the dinner and list the menu eaten on that occasion. Back in the 1970's and the 1980's French wines had not been discovered to a great extent in South Africa and for those in the know, one could quite easily obtain wines from Bordeaux or Burgundy. Seriously special lunches or dinners called for Domaine de la Romanée Conti, Château d'Yquem, Clos des Mouches and wonderful Bordeaux blends from Châteaux Calon Ségur, Gruaud Larose, Pavie and Haut-Batailley. Grand Crus Classés were readily available from Rebel and other liquor outlets in Durban.

From an early age my parents introduced us to home-grown fruit and vegetables and venison hunted on the farm. Growing up, we were taught to cook and appreciate food. When still quite little, Geneviève and I spent hours in restaurants trying to be as good as gold as our palates were developed to enjoy oysters, freshly caught stumpnose, snails and artichokes. All this, whilst younger sister Catherine's favourite order at Le St Geran was prawns! The wine and food education continued unabated. Classes were taken at Christina Martin's in Florida Road, which included a 40th birthday gift of a Weber and lessons on how to light a fire and braai to perfection! Trips overseas included visits to the Beaune cellars of Joseph Drouhin, lunches at L'Auberge de l'Ill in Illhaeusern in

France's Alsace region prepared by the Haeberlin brothers, Paul and Jean-Pierre and dinners at La Pomme d'Amour in London.

In 2006, my brother Vince ran the Marathon du Medoc and Francesco and I were part of the support team along with Maria, our sister-in-law and our cousins from Toulouse Marie-Anne, Pascal, Sandra and Guillaume. After sampling delicious Bordeaux specialities at Café Lavinal, Bistro of Château Lynch-Bages, we discovered to the north of Bordeaux and south of Pauillac, a very special place called Labat. The place name of this little hamlet on the ancient grounds of the Seigneurerie of St Maubert included a vineyard, which was first reported in the 18th century and is in the direct neighbourhood of Château Caronne Ste Gemme and various Cru Classés such as Lagrange & Gruaud Larose, situated nearby. Nowadays the hamlet is mainly populated by farmers. In 1900, ownership of Château Labat passed to the Nony family who still run the vineyard today.

Back in March 1998, Colleen and I toured Ireland armed with a B&B guide and the smallest hired car the Airport had on offer. We travelled 1,638 kms from Dublin to Connemara and back and thanks to Anne, we enjoyed the magic of St Patrick's Day, with cousin Oonagh, where the Liffey ran green and the colourful parade tripped past us as we clung to the pillars of Trinity College. One of our stops on this visit was at Ballymaloe Cookery School in Shanagarry, County Cork.

13 years later I had the privilege of spending 12 weeks as a Ballymaloe student with the

May 2011 intake. The 64 students at Ballymaloe hailed from 14 different nations. We learnt a lot about each others' food cultures and spent time exploring food markets, restaurants, sampling wild salmon and Dublin Bay prawns, freshly caught mackerel and being introduced to sherries from Spain, wines from Italy and Champagne from France. Ballymaloe demonstrated a holistic approach to farming and taught us to better understand the importance of local food suppliers and seasonal produce. This was my third visit to Ireland and my fascination with the Emerald Isle continues unabated.

My next book is in the planning stages and will be a tribute to my roots in Mauritius. I have called the 2nd book, Palm Hearts and Pineapples. It is a nod to La Martinière, the farm in the deep south of the Island, where my father, Maurice and his siblings, Tonton Jacques, Tante Liline, Tante Monique and Jano grew up.

Enjoy this collection of recipes and remember life is for living!

Seasonal fruits and vegetables in South Africa

SPRING FRUIT Sep, Oct, Nov	SUMMER FRUIT Dec, Jan, Feb	AUTUMN FRUIT Mar, Apr, May	WINTER FRUIT Jun, Jul, Aug
Apples	Apricots	Apples	Apples
Avocados	Bananas	Avocados	Avocados
Bananas	Blackberries	Figs	Dates
Gooseberries	Cherries	Granadillas	Grapefruit
Coconuts	Figs	Grapefruit	Lemons
Dates	Grapes	Grapes	Limes
Grapefruit	Guavas	Lemons	Melon
Guavas	Lemons	Naartjies	Naartjies
Lemons	Litchis	Oranges	Oranges
Naartjies	Mangoes	Papayas	Papayas
Nectarines	Melon	Pears	Pears
Oranges	Mulberries	Pineapples	Pineapples
Papaya	Nectarines	Plums	
Pears	Papayas	Pomegranates	
Pineapples	Peaches	Quinces	
Sweet melon	Pineapples	Sweet melon	
Strawberries	Plums	Watermelon	
	Pomegranates		
November	Prunes		
Apricots	Quinces		
Blackberries	Raspberries		
Cherries	Strawberries		
Plums	Sweet melon		
Prunes	Watermelon		
Raspberries			
Sweet melon			
Watermelon			

SPRING VEGGIES	SUMMER VEGGIES	AUTUMN VEGGIES	WINTER VEGGIES
Artichokes	Artichokes	Aubergines	Asparagus
Asparagus	Asparagus	Baby marrows	Beetroot
Aubergines	Aubergines	Beetroot	Broad beans
Baby marrows	Baby marrows	Broad beans	Broccoli
Beetroot	Beetroot	Broccoli	Brussel sprouts
Brussels sprouts	Chives	Brussel sprouts	Fennel
Kale spinach	Green beans	Butter beans	Kale spinach
Maize	Maize	Parsnips	Parsnips
Parsnips	Patty pans	Radishes	Pumpkin
Red onions	Radishes	Sweet peppers	Radishes
Rhubarb	Red onions	Turnips	Turnips
Turnips	Rhubarb		Watercress
Watercress			

Local suppliers

Support your Local Food Suppliers and Farmers' Markets to ensure you know the source of your food. I have included a list of our favourites at the front of the book for easy reference.

FOR BEEF, DUCK & LAMB
Hope Meat SupplieS
Vikki & Michael Ker-Fox
Shop 17A, Mackeurtan Ave
Durban North
Tel: 082 485 1009
www.hopemeats.co.za

COFFEE & TEA
Colombo Tea & Coffee Co.
Barbra Bowman
59 Adelaide Tambo Drive
Durban North
Tel: 031 205 3283
www.colombo.co.za

FOR PORK
Dargle Valley Pork Products
Caz Griffin
Tel: 082 457 0987
Fax: 086 540 2854
Email: info@darglevalleypork.co.za
www.darglevalleypork.co.za

FISH & SEAFOOD
Bartho's Fish Company
Daryl and Brett Bartho
Shop 12D, Mackeurtan Avenue
Durban North
Tel: 031 563 7534
www.barthos.co.za

ITALIAN & FRENCH DELI PRODUCTS
Adriatic Ship Supply & Trading Co.
Wally Chelini
10, Davenport Avenue
Glenwood
Durban
Tel: 031 201 3123
www.adriatic.co.za

WINES
Marriott Gardens Liquor Store
Herve Allen
Shop 3, Cowey House
136 Problem Mkhize Road (Previously Cowey)
Durban
Tel: 031 309 2079
Email: herveallen@hotmail.com

DELI & RESTAURANT
Sprigs: The Food Shop
Fiona and Clare Ras
Fields Shopping Centre
Old Main Road, Kloof
Tel: 031 764 6031
www.sprigs.co.za

STRAWBERRY SUPPLIER
Cappeny Estates
Yoliswa and Bongani Gumede
D176 off Esenembe Road Compensation, Ballito
Tel: 032 815 1168
Tel: 083 659 0244
www.cappenyestates.com

FARMERS' MARKETS

Shongweni Farmers' Market
Christine Standeaven
Lot 457
Mr551 Shongweni
Tel: 083 777 1674
www.shongwenimarket.co.za

The Litchi Orchard
Seaforth Farm
Seaforth Avenue
Salt Rock
Tel: 032 525 5118
www.litchiorchard.co.za

SEASONING & COCONUT OIL PRODUCTS

Imbali Blends
Danielle Simpson
Tel: 082 820 0699
Danielle@imbaliblends.co.za
www.imbaliblends.co.za

Conversion charts

All recipes serve 8 persons unless otherwise specified. All spoon measures are level. All eggs used are large and free range where possible. Ovens and grills should be preheated to the specific temperature required as per recipe.

OVEN TEMPERATURES

°C (Centigrade)	°F (Fahrenheit)	Gas
110	225	¼
140	275	1
160	325	3
180	350	4
220	425	7
240	475	9

SMALL MEASURES

Metric	U.S.
1 ml	¼ tspn
2.5 ml	½ tspn
5 ml	1 tspn
15 ml	1 T (Tablespoon)

LIQUID MEASURES

Metric	Imperial	U.S.
60 ml	2 fl oz	¼ cup
125 ml	4 fl oz	½ cup
250 ml	8 fl oz	1 cup
300 ml	10 fl oz / ½ pint	1 ¼ cups
625 ml	20 fl oz / 1 pint	2 ½ cups
1 litre	35 fl oz	1 quart / 4 cups

DRY MEASURES

Metric	Imperial
25 g	1 oz
50 g	2 oz
100 g	4 oz
225 g	8 oz
500 g	1 lb 2 oz
900 g	2 lbs
1.3 kg	3 lbs

LENGTHS

Metric	Imperial
5 mm	¼ inch
1 cm	½ inch
2.5 cm	1 inch
10 cm	4 inch
15 cm	6 inch
30 cm	12 inch

Breads and biscuits

14

Ciabatta

Makes 2 loaves

Our household comprises Italian and French Mauritian heritage. One thing we have in common is our love of bread. The smell of freshly baked bread evokes childhood memories and good times. It provides comfort and sustenance. Ciabatta has an open texture characteristic and dunking the bread into a bowl of warmed Extra Virgin olive oil to eat with a green salad is simply heavenly.

Start by making the bread starter the previous day.

3.5 g fresh yeast or ½ tspn dried yeast
288 g organic white bread flour
200 ml warm filtered water

Measure the 200 ml of warm water in a jug. In a small bowl, mix the fresh yeast with a little of the warm water. Mix all the bread starter ingredients together in a large bowl. Mix all the ingredients with your hands. You should feel the elasticity as the gluten develops in the bread starter. Cover the bowl with cling film and leave it to stand at room temperature for between 12 and 24 hours.

3.5 g fresh yeast or ½ tspn dried yeast
250 g organic white bread flour
7.5 g sea salt
250 g of the bread starter you started making the day before
150 ml warm water
Extra Virgin olive oil

Measure 150ml of warm water into a jug. In a small bowl, mix the yeast and 1 ½ T of the warm water. Combine the flour and the salt in the bowl of your mixer. Add the bread starter, the yeast liquid and the warm water. Use your mixer to knead the dough until it is elastic. If the dough can be stretched without tearing or breaking then you have achieved the elasticity required. Oil a large bowl and add the dough. Gently turn the dough in the bowl until it is covered in olive oil. Leave it in a warm place to rise until it has doubled in size, approximately 2 hours.

Oil a large baking tray. Flour a large working surface. Gently put the puffed up dough onto the floured surface trying not to knock the dough down. Flour your hands and using a dough scraper or sharp knife, cut the dough into two pieces. Roll each piece of dough into the flour and stretch it into an elongated shape and place each one onto the baking tray. Cover the loaves with a clean, dry tea towel and leave to prove for a further hour.

Preheat your oven to 200°C or 180°C fan. The loaves will still look flat after the proving process, however they will spring up in the oven. Bake the ciabatta loaves for 20 minutes until each is golden brown. Cool the loaves on a wire rack. It is best to wait until the loaves have cooled down before slicing the bread. If not you may end up with a very flattened ciabatta slice.

Beer loaf

Makes 1 loaf

A very simple, foolproof bread recipe that can be rustled up at short notice.

500 g self-raising flour
350 ml beer
Sea salt, freshly ground black pepper, ½ tspn powdered English mustard
Mix in any savoury items such as grated onion, cheese, chopped tomatoes, mixed herbs etc.

Preheat your oven to 220°C.
Mix all the ingredients together to form a thick dough. Pour the dough into a buttered loaf tin measuring 23 cm x 12 cm. Place in the hot oven and bake for 10 – 15 minutes. Reduce the heat to 150°C and continue baking for a further 35 minutes. You can check for doneness whilst the bread is baking as this loaf will not flop!

Cheese and onion loaf
Makes 1 loaf

My Aunt Odile gave me this recipe many years ago and it's perfect to serve at a braai!

360 g self-raising flour
2 T sugar
3 T finely chopped onion
1 tspn dried mixed herbs
1 cup grated mature Cheddar cheese
350 ml beer

Preheat your oven to 120°C.
Combine the flour, sugar, onion, herbs and grated cheese in a large bowl. Stir in the beer and turn into a well-greased loaf tin measuring 23 cm x 12 cm. Place the loaf tin in the pre-heated oven and cook for 50 minutes or until a skewer when inserted into the centre of the bread comes out clean. Remove from the oven and stand on a wire rack for 5 minutes. Then turn out the loaf and cool on the wire rack.

Health bread
Makes 1 loaf

Decorating the health bread with sesame and poppy seeds gives this loaf a beautiful finish!

2 cups nutty wheat flour
1 cup stoneground bread flour
2 tspn brown sugar
2 cups plain full cream yoghurt
1 T sesame seeds

1 cup cake flour, sifted
1 heaped tspn sea salt
2 tspn bicarbonate of soda
1 T full cream free-range cow's milk
1 T poppy seeds

Preheat the oven to 180°C.
Mix all the dry ingredients together and stir well. Blend the bicarbonate of soda into the yoghurt with a tablespoon of milk. Add the yoghurt to the dry ingredients. Put the dough into a greased loaf tin, sprinkle with sesame seeds and poppy seeds. Bake for 90 minutes.

Seed loaf
Makes 1 loaf

Buttermilk is readily available in South Africa. If you're out of buttermilk, simply add 1 tablespoon of freshly squeezed lemon juice to 1 cup of milk as a substitute.

1 cup coconut flour
1 cup mixed seeds (Chia, Flax, Poppy, Pumpkin, Sesame, Sunflower)
¼ cup psyllium husks
2 tspn baking powder
1 tspn salt
6 large free-range eggs
1 cup buttermilk

Preheat the oven to 180°C.
Line the bottom of a regular loaf tin (21 cm x 11 cm) with baking paper. Grease the sides with coconut oil. Mix all the dry ingredients including the seeds. Break 6 eggs into a Pyrex jug and beat lightly. Add the buttermilk. Add to dry ingredients and mix gently. Pour the mixture into the loaf tin. Bake in pre-heated oven at 180°C for 55 minutes.

Wholewheat loaf

Makes 1 loaf

If you enjoy bread and collecting bread recipe books don't miss out on *Crust: Bread to get your teeth into* by Richard Bertinet. *Dough* was the title of Richard's first book and it has won the Guild of Food Writers' Award for Best First Book. Then there's my favourite, *The Bread Baker's Apprentice: Mastering the art of extraordinary bread* by Peter Reinhart. Another one of Peter's bread books is *Artisan Breads every Day: Fast and Easy recipes for world-class breads*. By comparison to those recipes, this wholewheat loaf is very simple to produce. Enjoy your bread baking!

600 g organic wholewheat flour
2 tspn sea salt
1 T organic butter, melted
850 ml lukewarm water
20 g yeast

290 g cake flour
1 large egg, beaten
1 T white sugar
30 g sunflower seeds

Preheat the oven to 200°C. Prepare the yeast beforehand. Mix 200 ml lukewarm water, the yeast and the sugar together and allow to ferment and rise. Place both flours into a large mixing bowl. In a smaller bowl mix the melted butter, egg, salt and the remainder of the lukewarm water. Add these wet ingredients to the bowl with the flours. Add the yeast mixture and the sunflower seeds. Stir well. Place in a medium sized loaf tin (23 cm x 13 cm) and cover with some wax paper. Place the loaf tin in a warm area and allow to rise slightly. Bake in the oven for 45 minutes or until the skewer comes out dry.

Date squares

Makes 20 squares

This is a very special treat loaded with sugar. Eat it sparingly.

1 cup Medjool dates, stoned and chopped
½ cup brown sugar
½ cup sugar
1 tspn vanilla extract
1 tspn baking powder
½ cup brown sugar

½ cup water
6 T butter
2 free range egg yolks
1 ½ cups cake flour, sifted
2 egg whites

Preheat the oven to 180ºC.

Butter and line a 20 cm square baking pan. In a saucepan boil the dates, water and 1st batch of brown sugar until the mixture thickens. Remove from heat and allow to cool. In a bowl, combine butter, 2nd batch of brown sugar and egg yolks. Add the vanilla extract, then the sifted dry ingredients. Pour the batter into the lined baking pan. Then spread the date mixture gently on top. In a separate bowl, beat the egg whites into stiff peaks and gently fold in the 3rd batch of brown sugar. Pour the brown sugar meringue over the date layer and bake for 45 minutes. To serve, cut into squares once cooled.

21

Dried oregano biscuits
Makes 24 biscuits

These savoury biscuits are vegan and are quick and easy to make with pantry ingredients.

2 cups almond flour
2 T dried oregano
2 T water

¾ tspn sea salt
1 T Extra Virgin olive oil

Preheat the oven to 170°C.

In a large bowl, combine the almond flour, the salt and the dried oregano. In a smaller bowl whisk together the olive oil and water. Stir the wet ingredients into the almond flour mixture until thoroughly combined. Roll the dough into a ball. Place a Silpat mat onto a large baking sheet. Place the dough in the middle of the mat and place a 2nd Silpat mat on top of the dough. Gently roll the dough to 3mm thickness using a rolling pin. Try to do this evenly and don't allow the edges to get too thin or they may burn. Remove the top Silpat mat. Score the dough using a pizza cutter or knife (without cutting through the Silpat mat) lengthwise into 4 sections, then across into 6 sections. Bake for 9-10 minutes until lightly golden. Cool on the tray with wire rack for about 20 minutes and serve with the aubergine pâté.

Dips

Artichoke and ricotta cheese dip

Serves 8

Since inception in December 1993, our Bookclub evenings were fun occasions to experiment especially for our vegetarian girlfriends. The combo of ingredients makes for a delicious dip.

4 marinated artichoke hearts, chopped
1 large bunch baby spinach, washed and chopped
½ cup ricotta cheese
3 T Pecorino cheese, grated
1 garlic clove, crushed
1 T freshly squeezed lemon juice
1 T Italian parsley, chopped
3 T Extra Virgin olive oil

Put the artichokes, baby spinach, garlic, lemon juice, Pecorino cheese and parsley in a food processor and pulse until finely chopped. Add the ricotta cheese and pulse to combine. Slowly add the olive oil until you have a smooth consistency. Season to taste. Put the artichoke and ricotta cheese dip into a serving bowl and drizzle with additional olive oil. Serve this dip with the Dried Oregano Biscuits.

Aubergine paté

Serves 8 as an amuse bouche

Wherever I have worked there has always been an opportunity to share food experiences and recipes. This Middle Eastern recipe was given to me by Nadia when we worked at the Durban Chamber of Commerce and Industry together.

1 large aubergine or two medium sized (also known as brinjal or eggplant)
3 T peanut butter
1 garlic clove, crushed
Sea salt
Extra Virgin olive oil

Juice of 1 lemon
bunch of Italian parsley, finely chopped
Freshly ground black pepper

Preheat the oven to 180°C.
To cook the aubergine, prick them in several places with a sharp knife. Bake the aubergine until soft, approximately 40 minutes. Scoop out the flesh and mash well using a fork. Add the peanut butter, lemon juice and crushed garlic and mix thoroughly. Add the remaining ingredients and mix once again. Drizzle some olive oil on top of the aubergine pâté and serve with crackers or toasted bread triangles. This aubergine pâté is also delicious served on slices of cucumber.

Caramalised onion and bacon dip
Serves 8 as an amuse bouche

Caramelised onions work beautifully in this dip and pairs well with the bacon.

1 T coconut oil
6 strips bacon, cooked and crumbled
250 g full cream cottage cheese
1 clove garlic, crushed
½ tspn sea salt

2 medium onions, finely diced
2 T bacon grease, reserved
1 tspn Worcestershire sauce
¼ tspn paprika
¼ tspn freshly ground black pepper

Heat the oil in a pan over medium heat. Add the onions and stir to coat. Cook the onions, stirring occasionally until they are evenly browned and caramelised, about 30 minutes. Let them cool. Place the remaining ingredients in a medium bowl and stir well to mix. Add the caramelised onions, mix to combine and serve with crackers or savoury biscuits of your choice.

Dukkah

The word is derived from Arabic meaning "to pound" since the mixture of spices and nuts are pounded together after being dry roasted. Dukkah is wonderful served with home-made ciabatta bread and a bowl of warmed Extra Virgin olive oil.

110 g hazelnuts
2 T coriander seeds
2 tspn freshly ground black pepper
Extra virgin olive oil, to serve

80 g sesame seeds
2 T cumin seeds
1 tspn flaked sea salt
Crusty bread, to serve

Preheat oven to 180°C. Spread the hazelnuts over a baking tray and cook in preheated oven for 3-4 minutes or until toasted. Rub the hazelnuts between a clean tea towel to remove as much skin as possible. Place the toasted hazelnuts in the bowl of a food processor and process until coarsely chopped. Transfer to a large bowl. Heat a medium frying pan over medium heat. Add the sesame seeds and cook, stirring, for 1-2 minutes or until golden. Add to the bowl with the hazelnuts. Place coriander seeds and cumin seeds in frying pan over medium heat, and cook, stirring frequently, for 1-2 minutes or until aromatic and seeds begin to pop. Transfer seeds to a mortar and pestle. Pound until finely crushed, alternatively, use a coffee or spice grinder. Add the crushed spices, pepper and salt to the hazelnut mixture and mix well.

Macadamia nut pesto

Down the South Coast where we grew up and went to school, live our farming friends Leanne and Bruce. The macadamia nuts grown on the farm are world class and am very grateful to Leanne for supplying me with this delicious produce for the Low Carb High Fat food demo done with banting specialist, Dr Glen Hagemann of Asset Health / Sharks Medical.

½ cup of raw macadamia nuts
2 cups young basil leaves
2 garlic cloves, chopped
¾ cup Parmigiano Reggiano cheese, freshly grated
½ lemon, freshly juiced
¼ cup of Extra Virgin olive oil
¼ teaspoon sea salt

In a food processor, using a pulse action, chop the macadamias, basil, garlic and Parmigiano Reggiano until very finely minced. Pulse in the lemon juice and olive oil. Add salt to taste. The mixture should be puréed, but retain some texture. Excellent with freshly cooked zucchini spirals or spread on a slice of seed loaf.

Mexican Guacamole

Serves 8

Guacamole is an avocado based dip. Avocado is incredibly nutritious. See page 129 for more on avocado.

3 ripe avocado
2 T freshly squeezed lemon juice
4 T Extra Virgin olive oil
2 garlic cloves, crushed
1 vine tomato or 4 small cherry tomatoes, finely chopped
1 tspn Tabasco sauce
Sea salt and freshly ground black pepper
5 spring onions, finely sliced
2 T Italian parsley, finely chopped

Halve the avocado, remove the pips, spoon the flesh into a bowl and add all the ingredients except seasoning, spring onions and parsley. Blend into a rough pulp. Season. Fold in the spring onions and parsley. Spoon into a serving bowl and serve with Dried Oregano Biscuits.

Peppadew® with goat's cheese, basil, chives
Makes 24

Sweet piquanté peppers are produced in the moderate to warmer climatic conditions of the Limpopo and Mpumalanga provinces of South Africa. These delicious peppers are a quick snack on their own or you can add goat's cheese for an extra dimension!

24 pickled peppadews®, drained
250 g soft goat's cheese log
50 g finely chopped chives
Small bunch of fresh basil leaves, washed and delicately dried

Drain the peppadews® and fill each one with the goat's cheese, using the back of a small coffee spoon. Place the finely chopped chives on a flat plate. Dip each peppadew® into the chives so that the goat's cheese is covered. Tuck a small basil leaf into the goats' cheese very gently. The filled peppadews® may be covered and refrigerated for up to 2 hours before serving.

Salads, sambals and dressings

Coconut and tamarind chutney

This sambal pairs beautifully with the Mauritian chicken and prawn curry and is my all-time favourite. We have a wonderful saying in South Africa "some PT is involved", physical training as the fresh coconut pieces are grated by hand and depending on how many your curry is catering for, this might take you a little while but the results and compliments will be worth it!

250 g fresh coconut pieces, grated
1 small knob of fresh ginger, grated
1 garlic clove, crushed
1 tspn apple cider vinegar
1 T Extra Virgin olive oil
1 small green chilli, seeds removed and finely chopped
1 T seedless tamarind, available from specialist Asian shops or pick a ripe pod off your tree if you live in Mauritius!

Mix the tamarind pulp with the Apple Cider vinegar to loosen the pulp and then add all the other ingredients. Enjoy the sambal with your curry!

Mozzarella and roast red pepper salad
Serves 8

Woolworths' *Taste* magazine ran a competition in August 2011 asking readers to send in their best recipes, best wines and favourite restaurants. Francesco and I were on Capri off the Amalfi Coast when I received a telephone call from Cape Town advising that I had won the favourite reader recipe and my dish would appear on the cover of the November 2011 edition of Taste magazine. It was all very exciting for this Facebook Foodie!

8 red peppers
6 garlic cloves, thinly sliced
8 plum tomatoes
4 x 250 g buffalo mozzarella
edible flowers to garnish

8 T Extra Virgin olive oil
300 g cherry tomatoes
2 T red wine vinegar
bunch of basil leaves

Preheat the oven to 200°C. Halve the peppers and remove the seeds. Drizzle with 4 T olive oil, scatter over the garlic and season. Roast for 30 – 40 minutes. Toss the cherry tomatoes in 2 T olive oil, season and add to the peppers for the last 10 minutes of the roasting time. Halve the plum tomatoes, squeeze out the seeds and juice and then halve again. Plate with the roast peppers and cherry tomatoes. Whisk the remaining olive oil and red wine vinegar. Drizzle over the salad, top with the mozzarella and edible flowers.

Asian chicken salad

Serves 8

Start this recipe the day before. It's a great dish for entertaining large crowds and can be easily doubled or trebled.

1.6 kg chicken breasts, flattened
¾ cup Tamari
¾ cup dry Sherry
1 ½ T ginger, grated on a Micro-plane
3 cloves garlic, crushed

Place the flattened chicken breasts in a glass dish. Mix the marinade ingredients and coat the chicken pieces with the marinade. Cover the bowl with cling film and refrigerate overnight.

The next day prepare the dressing.

Dressing

1 cup Extra Virgin olive Oil
¾ cup dry white wine
¼ cup sugar
2 T Tamari
½ tspn mustard powder
Black pepper

To cook the chicken

¾ cup cornflour
¾ cup cake flour
½ cup finely slice spring onions
1 cup toasted slivered almonds
6 baby gem lettuces, washed, spun dry and torn

Mix the cornflour and the cake flour. Drain the chicken pieces from the marinade. Roll the chicken pieces in the flour to coat lightly. Fry the chicken pieces in Extra Virgin olive oil until lightly browned and cooked. Drain chicken pieces on paper towels. Allow to cool. Cut the chicken into bite-sized pieces. Toss the chicken, spring onions and slivered almonds gently together. Serve on a bed of rocket.

Nectarine, rocket, walnut and ginger salad

Serves 8

Back in February 2012, one of my close friends challenged me on Facebook to produce a strawberry, balsamic and black pepper ice cream. For the dinner, I served this salad as a starter on that fun evening! If you would like to serve this salad as part of a vegan dinner, simply replace the honey with organic maple syrup.

1 lime
½ tspn chilli flakes
2 T of the ginger syrup
2 T avocado oil
Freshly ground black pepper
4 T walnuts
1 loaf Italian ciabatta bread

2 tspn honey
1 knob ginger in syrup
2 T Extra Virgin olive oil
Sea salt
8 nectarines
150 g rocket leaves
1 garlic clove, crushed

Vinaigrette

Zest and juice the lime into a mixing bowl and lightly whisk in the honey, chilli flakes, chopped ginger, the ginger syrup, olive oil, avocado oil, salt and pepper. Stone and quarter the fruit and marinate in the dressing for 30 minutes. When ready to serve, toast walnuts and add with the rocket to the fruit. Toast slices of bread, drizzle with a little Extra Virgin olive oil and rub with garlic. Top each slice with a handful of salad.

Pineapple, cucumber, red onion and chilli salsa
Serves 8

At *La Martinière*, our family farm in Mauritius, Papa grows the sweetest pineapple imaginable. This salsa works well with braaied pork cutlets.

1 pineapple, peeled, eyes removed and diced
1 large English cucumber, peeled and diced
1 red onion sliced finely
1 large red chilli
1 bunch coriander, washed and torn
1 bunch chives, sliced finely

Salsa Dressing
2 T freshly squeezed lime juice
1 T Tamari

1 T rice vinegar
2 T Extra Virgin olive oil

Combine all salad ingredients. Combine ingredients for the dressing in a glass jar. Close the lid and give the jar a good shake to combine all the ingredients. Drizzle over the salsa and serve.

Prawn salad with French coarse grain mustard dressing

Serves 8

The taste of French coarse grain mustard enhances this dish to form a delicious sauce for the prawns. I have included two of my favourite vinaigrettes below for you to enjoy.

40 medium prawns, deveined and shelled
2 T French coarse grain mustard
1 T butter
Lettuce leaves, washed and dried
Mix of fresh herbs for garnish

3 T white wine
½ cup cream
1 T avocado oil
French vinaigrette

Sauté the prawns in the hot oil and butter mix. When lightly cooked, remove from the pan and deglaze the pan with the white wine. Add the mustard and the cream and allow to reduce over low heat. Return the prawns to the pan and remove from heat. Mix the lettuce leaves in a large bowl, season, add a little French vinaigrette and toss carefully. Arrange the lettuce on the individual serving plates and spoon the prawns on the side of the salad. Garnish with fresh herbs and serve.

French Vinaigrette

1 shallot, finely diced
1 tspn Dijon mustard
Fleur de Sel

2 T red wine vinegar
8 T Extra Virgin olive oil
Freshly ground black pepper

Put the finely chopped shallot into a small glass jar. Add the red wine vinegar and allow to steep for 5 minutes. Add the salt, a little freshly ground black pepper and the Dijon mustard, stir well and then add the olive oil. Close the jar with a tight fitting lid and give the jar a few vigorous shakes. Check for seasoning.

Mauritian Vinaigrette

This keeps very well in the fridge for up to a week.

1 hard boiled egg, large and free range
1 tspn Dijon mustard
Fleur de Sel

2 T white wine vinegar
8 T Extra Virgin olive oil
Freshly ground black pepper

Separate the hard boiled yolk from the hard boiled white of the egg. Mash the hard boiled egg yolk. Into a glass jar place the salt, pepper, mashed egg yolk and Dijon mustard. Mix well with a teaspoon. Add the vinegar. Close the jar with a tight fitting lid and give the jar a few vigourous shakes to combine these ingredients. Add the olive oil to the jar. Mix to combine. Slice the hard-boiled egg white and add to your vinaigrette. Serve with your favourite salad greens.

Salad of Tenderstem broccoli with goat's cheese and chilli flakes

Serves 8

Francesco and I took this salad to Seula Zimbili, situated in the Harold Johnson Nature Reserve on the banks of the mighty Tugela River for a Rotary Club function. Seula Zimbili is run by Wally's parents, Lydia and William. The rains had fallen that morning and we forded a small stream to reach the venue. The salad worked well with the braai, our traditional South African barbecue!

6 T Extra Virgin olive oil for frying
4 cloves of garlic, crushed
200 g pecan nuts, shelled
½ tspn chilli flakes
Fleur de Sel

1 homemade ciabatta loaf, cut into small chunks
500 g Tenderstem broccoli, sliced into 5 cm
2 x 100 g goat's cheese logs
zest of 1 lemon
freshly ground black pepper

Place a non-stick pan over medium heat. Add 2 T Extra Virgin olive oil and fry the ciabatta chunks gently, turning until golden. Remove and drain on paper towel. Add another 2 T Extra Virgin olive oil and gently fry the garlic and pecans. Remove from pan and put on a plate. In the same pan, add the final 2 T olive oil and stir-fry the chilli flakes and Tenderstem broccoli until crunchy and still bright green. Allow to cool.

Place all the ingredients, except the goat's cheese and lemon zest, in a large flat serving platter. Once all the ingredients have been placed on the serving platter, add the goat's cheese to the salad and sprinkle the salad with the lemon zest.

Roasted tomato chutney

This tomato chutney is a delicious accompaniment to curry and in Mauritius we roast the tomatoes to extract maximum flavour. When we came home from school in the afternoons, one of our favourite snacks was toasted bread spread with butter and peanut-butter and topped with the tomato chutney.

2 large ripe tomatoes
1 small knob of grated ginger
Fleur de Sel and freshly ground black pepper

1 small shallot, finely chopped
1 small garlic clove, peeled and crushed
Extra Virgin olive oil to drizzle

Preheat the oven to 200°C. Place the tomatoes on an oven tray and roast the tomatoes until they blister and the skins blacken. When cool enough to handle, peel the tomatoes. Chop finely. Add the chopped shallots, ginger, garlic. Season with salt and pepper. Taste and check the seasoning. Then drizzle a little Extra Virgin olive oil and serve with the curry of your choice.

Vegetable achards (or pickles)

The best way to prepare this delicious sambal is to chop all the vegetables according to the recipe and then to lay the chopped vegetables on clean trays in the sun to dry. Turn the vegetables two or three times throughout the day. Make a large batch of vegetable achards and store them in glass jars, in the refrigerator.

12 medium sized carrots, peeled and cut into julienne
1 large cauliflower, broken into florets
1 medium sized cabbage, finely sliced
500 g fine green beans, cut in half
1 large onion or 2 medium sized onions, sliced
125 g fresh ginger, peeled and grated
10 garlic cloves, peeled and crushed
4 T white spirit vinegar
2 T turmeric powder
200 ml coconut oil
1 large green chilli, deseeded and chopped
Sea salt and freshly ground black pepper

To sterilise the jars in which you will store the achards or pickles, wash the glass jars and dry them thoroughly. Then place the glass jars in the oven at 180°C for 15 minutes until they have been completely sterilised. Remember that your glass jars should have a non-reactive plastic coating inside the lid to avoid corrosion by the vinegar. Glass is also a perfect recyclable container.

To prepare the achards, heat the coconut oil in a large saucepan and add the turmeric powder. Stir continuously until the turmeric has melted. Add the white spirit vinegar and stir further. Then add the sliced onions, the chopped chilli, crushed garlic and the grated ginger. Gently sauté these ingredients until the onions have taken on the bright yellow colour of the tumeric. In order for the vegetables to retain their crunch, quickly add the carrots, cauliflower, cabbage and green beans and cook them for about 5 – 7 minutes. Remove from heat and allow to cool. Once cool, ladle the vegetables achards into the sterilized jars, seal and refrigerate. Prior to serving the vegetable achards, remove the jar from the fridge and allow to come to room temperature.

Soups

I am a big fan of soup. It probably stems from Père Paul, my maternal grandfather, who drank soup every evening at the start of his dinner. We watched with fascination when he would add a teaspoon of Lea & Perrins ® Worcestershire Sauce into his clear soup. There is nothing more satisfying than homemade chicken and vegetable soup. For this, a pressure cooker is a very versatile kitchen appliance that radically cuts down the cooking time for your soup as well as your energy bill!

Chicken and vegetable soup

Serves 8

1 chicken carcass
1 large onion
2 sprigs parsley
5 whole black peppercorns

2 medium carrots
2 stalks celery
1 bay leaf

Put the chicken carcass into the pressure cooker pot. Add all the vegetables and the whole black peppercorns. Cover the chicken carcass and vegetables with filtered cold water. Close the pressure cooker pot as per instructions. Bring up to pressure on high heat then reduce heat to low and cook for 30 minutes. Remove the pressure cooker from the stove. Allow all the steam to dissipate before opening the lid according to the pressure cooker manual instructions and enjoy!

Broccoli and feta cheese soup

Serves 8

450 g broccoli
450 g potatoes
50 g butter
2 litres organic chicken stock
salt and pepper to taste
200 g feta cheese
1 cup full cream milk
¼ cup cream

Wash the broccoli well and cut into bite-sized pieces. Peel and slice the potatoes, melt the butter and sauté broccoli and potatoes. Add the chicken stock, salt and pepper and bring to the boil. Then simmer for about 20 minutes or until vegetables are soft. Purée the soup in batches, adding the feta cheese gradually in the process. Return to the pot, add milk and cream and reheat. Check seasoning and serve with slices of freshly made health bread.

Cream of mushroom soup

Serves 8

This recipe was copied onto a piece of paper whilst sitting on the beach at Les Salines in Black River, Mauritius in the company of my sister, Catherine and her husband Gérald. It was a Saturday the 28th July many years ago and Caliph the family hound was enjoying his swim in the sea! The recipe came via our sister Geneviève. It had been given to Geneviève by her Scottish friend Paula. The original recipe called for potato and here I have substituted sweet potato.

1 large onion, finely chopped
250 g large brown mushrooms, sliced thinly
4 T organic butter
1 large orange sweet potato, peeled and chopped
1 tspn fresh thyme
1 tspn fresh Italian parsley, chopped
3 cups free-range cow's milk

Melt the butter in a heavy based saucepan and fry the onions until golden. Add the chopped sweet potato and mushrooms and sauté for about 3 minutes. Add remaining ingredients and slowly bring to the boil. Simmer for about 15 minutes. Taste and adjust seasoning if necessary. Allow to cool slightly. Remove the thyme sprigs and then purée the soup until smooth. Serve in warm bowls with slices of homemade bread.

Hearty potato soup

Serves 8

1 kg potatoes
2 spring onions, sliced
1 T organic butter
1 bay leaf
2 large sprigs of parsley, chopped

2 litres organic chicken stock
2 onions, chopped
1 T Extra Virgin olive oil
1 smoked sausage, such as chorizo

Peel and slice the potatoes and cook in the chicken stock until they disintegrate. Using a handheld masher, mash the potato in the stock. In a separate pan, melt the butter and the oil until hot and sauté the chopped vegetables for a couple of minutes. Add the chopped vegetables and bay leaf to the soup pan and simmer for 30 minutes. Remove the bay leaf. Add slices of smoked sausage to the soup. Ladle the soup into warmed bowls and garnish with chopped parsley.

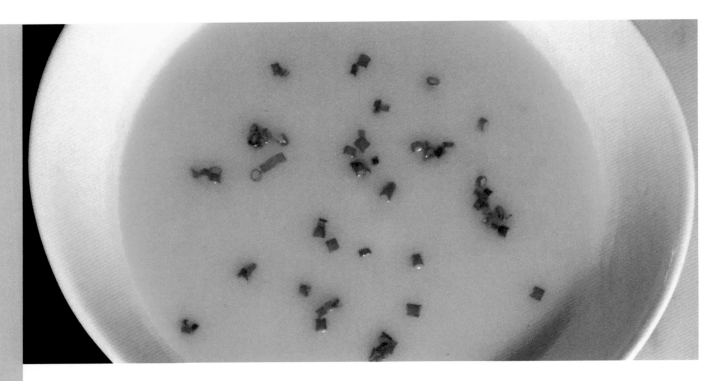

Cream of butternut soup

Serves 8

Butternut squash is a magical vegetable. It works beautifully as a roasted and caramelised vegetable accompaniment to grilled meats, it is silky smooth in soup, makes for perfect Paleo pasta and is irresistible cold in salads with feta cheese and nuts!

2 T Extra Virgin olive oil
1 onion, finely chopped
2 sticks celery, chopped
500 g butternut squash, cubed (peeled weight)
1 medium orange sweet potato, peeled and cubed
½ tspn ground ginger
1 bay leaf
1 cup organic or free range cow's milk
To garnish: chopped chives

2 tspn butter
3 leeks, white parts only, chopped
4 cups homemade chicken stock
½ tspn salt
½ tspn turmeric
1 stick cinnamon
2 T sweet sherry

Heat the oil and the butter in a large saucepan. Add onion, leeks, celery, butternut and sweet potato. Cover the saucepan and sweat over low heat for about 10 minutes, stirring occasionally to prevent catching. Add all remaining ingredients except the milk and sherry. Bring to the boil; then cover and simmer gently until vegetables are soft. Remove the cinnamon stick and bay leaf and cool the soup a little. Purée the soup mixture in a blender in batches until smooth. Refrigerate the soup at this stage if you wish to make it in advance, even the day before.

To serve the soup, remove from the refrigerator 30 minutes before serving. Stir in the milk and reheat gently preferably in a double boiler, then stir in the sweet sherry. Taste the soup to check the seasoning. Ladle the soup into warmed soup bowls, sprinkle with the chopped chives. Serve with hot slices of seed loaf.

Cream of pear and watercress soup
Serves 8

8 ripe pears
1 litre homemade chicken stock
25 g watercress
Freshly ground black pepper
Sea salt
30 g blue cheese, crumbled
150 ml organic fresh cream
30 ml freshly squeezed lemon juice

Peel and core the pears. Cut into quarters. Place the chicken stock, pears and watercress in a heavy based pan and simmer until the pears are soft, approximately 10 minutes. Add the blue cheese and simmer until melted. Purée the soup with a stick blender or in a liquidiser. If you wish to serve this soup hot, then add the lemon juice and fresh cream and heat the soup very gently before serving in warmed bowls. If you wish to serve this soup cold, add the lemon juice and whisk the cream into the soup. Chill the soup until ready to serve cold.

Cream of spinach soup

Serves 8

One of my favourite dishes is wilted spinach served with boiled egg. This hot cream of spinach soup is filling and nutritious. We enjoy it in the colder months of the year.

900 g fresh spinach
300 ml double cream
Juice of ½ lemon
Freshly ground black pepper
1 large boiled egg, finely chopped for the garnish

4 T organic butter
400 ml homemade chicken stock
Sea salt

Wash the spinach leaves in several changes of cold water. Remove any tough stems. Drain well in a colander. Press out the excess moisture. Chop the leaves roughly. Melt the butter in a heavy based saucepan. Add the chopped spinach leaves and simmer gently, stirring occasionally for about 8 minutes or until the spinach is soft. Purée the spinach with a stick blender or in a liquidiser. Pour the spinach purée back into the heavy based pan that has been rinsed out. Stir in the cream and dilute to taste with the homemade chicken stock. Heat the soup through over moderate heat, stirring constantly. Season to taste with a little lemon juice, salt and freshly ground black pepper. Ladle into warmed soup bowls and garnish each portion with a sprinkling of the chopped boiled egg.

Gazpacho — a delicious cold Spanish soup
Serves 8

If there is one soup that is perfect on our hot summer days in Durban, it's a chilled gazpacho.

1 kg fresh ripe vine tomatoes, skinned and coarsely chopped
1 English cucumber, peeled and coarsely chopped
1 red pepper, seeded and coarsely chopped
½ onion, chopped
10 sprigs parsley, chopped
2 slices ciabatta bread, cubed
½ cup cold water
2 T Apple cider vinegar
Freshly ground black pepper

1 stalk celery, chopped
2 cloves garlic, crushed
2 T tomato puree
4 T Extra Virgin olive oil
2 tspn Sea salt

Place all the ingredients in a food processor and blend until the mixture is smooth and thick. Check the seasoning. Chill in the refrigerator for two hours before serving in chilled bowls. Serve this cold Spanish soup with all or a few of the following toppings: chopped Kalamata olives, chopped chives or finely chopped cucumber.

Sweetcorn soup

Serves 8

My great aunt Mithé Bax made this delicious soup many times for us in winter. Tante Mithé was my paternal grandmother's sister and lived in Australia, South Africa and Mauritius. We used to love listening to the stories she recounted as she had a wonderful sense of humour and loved nothing better than sharing the escapades and tricks of the younger nieces and nephews, our cousins, when we stayed in her home.

6 sweetcorn cobs
1 T organic butter
Sea salt

3 cups free-range full cream cow's milk
1 tspn cake flour
Freshly ground black pepper

Grate the sweetcorn kernels. In a medium sized pot, heat the milk and add the grated sweetcorn kernels. In another pan, melt the butter, take the pan off the heat and add the flour. Stir vigorously and return the pan to the stove to cook the flour and butter to make a roux. When the roux has cooked for a couple of minutes, slowly pour the hot milk and sweetcorn onto the roux and stir well over gentle heat for a further 5 minutes. Season the soup and serve in warmed bowls with slices of homemade bread and farm butter.

Beef

Asian style fillet of beef

Serves 8

One of my favourite restaurants in Durban was called Landau's. It was owner managed and operated by Penny and Edward Landau in what is now Joop's. Edward ran a cookery class over several weeks at the end of 1992, which I attended with good friend Rozzie. Edward's attention to detail, especially when preparing meat, was impeccable. When cooking this fillet of beef it is better to roast the fillet at a high temperature for a shorter period of time if you like your beef rare. Always remember that when carving beef, it should first be allowed to rest because upon relaxing some of the moisture is reabsorbed into the meat tissue. A good knife will also save precious juices as sawing away has the effect of compressing the tissue and squeezing out the moisture.

We buy our beef, lamb and duck at Hope Meat Supplies in Durban North from Vikki and Micky Ker-Fox. The beef is reared on family farms in Richmond and Underberg. The cattle are free to roam and graze wherever they please, which creates a natural and stress-free environment for the animals. Start this recipe the day before so that the marinade infuses the fillet of beef with flavour.

Marinade

1.6 kg fillet of beef	30 ml Maille Dijon mustard
30 ml Tamari sauce	15 ml Extra Virgin olive oil

Place the fillet of beef into a glass dish. Mix the mustard, Tamari and olive oil in a small bowl until well combined. Pour this marinade over the beef fillet, cover and refrigerate overnight.

Method

30 ml Extra Virgin olive oil	30 ml free-range butter
75 ml water	120 ml Balsamic vinegar
Fleur de Sel	

The next day remove the fillet of beef from the fridge 1 hour before cooking so that it returns to almost room temperature. When you are ready to cook the fillet, preheat the oven to 190°C.

Put a large pan onto the stove plate. Add the olive oil and once the oil is very hot, sear the fillet of beef all over for approximately 3 minutes. Then add the butter to the hot pan. Baste the fillet with the melted butter for a couple of minutes. Put the seared fillet onto an oven tray. Sprinkle some sea salt onto the beef and roast for 16 minutes if your preference is rare.

Whilst the fillet is cooking in the oven, turn the heat up under the large pan in which you seared the fillet, and add the water. Stir vigorously, scraping the bottom of the pan. Add the Balsamic vinegar. Turn the heat down under the pan and allow to simmer gently for 5 minutes. The sauce can be kept warm whilst the fillet is cooking. Take the fillet out of the oven once the desired cooking time has been reached. Cover the fillet loosely with aluminium foil and allow it to rest for 10 minutes. Slice the fillet into 16 thick slices and plate two slices per person. We like to serve this fillet of beef with a cauliflower purée and sautéed fine green beans.

Olive beef fillets

Serves 8

8 beef fillet steaks weighing 150 g each
400 ml organic beef stock
150 g Kalamata olives, stoned and crushed
150 ml dry red wine
6 T butter
Sea salt
150 g pine kernels, dry toasted

In a saucepan combine the beef stock, olives and wine. Bring to the boil and simmer for a few minutes, then keep warm whilst preparing the steaks. Toast the pine kernels in a small non-stick pan until lightly browned. Melt butter in a heavy pan such as the Le Creuset cast iron square skillet grill, which measures 26 cm. Fry steaks to your liking. Season the steaks with sea salt. Let the first batch of four steaks rest, covered with aluminium foil for five minutes whilst you cook the second batch of steaks. Once all eight steaks have been cooked, place them in a serving dish and pour the wine sauce over. Sprinkle with toasted pine kernels to garnish and serve with vegetables of your choice.

Chicken

Coconut cream and lime chicken

Serves 8

Tastes of Asia shine through in this pairing of coconut and lime.

1 kg chicken thigh fillets, deboned
4 cloves garlic, crushed
8 tspn finely grated ginger, use a Micro-plane
4 tspn finely grated lime zest
5 T freshly squeezed lime juice
8 tspn fish sauce
650 ml coconut cream
Garnish with coriander leaves

Combine the garlic, ginger, lime zest and juice, fish sauce and coconut cream in a Pyrex jug. Place the chicken high fillets in an ovenproof dish. Pour the marinade over the chicken and refrigerate for 30 minutes. Preheat your oven to 180°C. Remove the chicken from the refrigerator. Bake the chicken for 30 minutes. Serve the coconut cream and lime chicken with cauliflower rice and pan fried green beans. Garnish with fresh coriander leaves.

Chicken casserole

Serves 8

Chicken is extremely versatile and this casserole cooks quickly!

16 free range deboned chicken thighs
4 stalks celery, finely chopped
1 punnet button mushrooms
2 T Extra Virgin olive oil
Finely chopped parsley to garnish

3 medium onions, chopped
4 medium carrots, thinly sliced
5 T butter
1 cup organic home-made chicken stock
Sea salt and freshly ground black pepper

Over medium heat melt the butter in a deep thick bottomed pan and add the olive oil. Turn the heat to low, add the chicken pieces and brown the chicken, until lightly brown all over about 8-10 minutes. Watch carefully that the chicken does not burn. Add the chopped onion, carrots and celery and continue to cook on low heat for a further 5 minutes. Add the button mushrooms and chicken stock and stir. Continue cooking on low heat uncovered for further 10 minutes until the vegetables are firm but not soft and the mushrooms are cooked through. Taste for seasoning and add a little sea salt and freshly ground black pepper.
Serve the casserole on cauliflower mash or sweet potato mash. Sprinkle the chicken with finely chopped parsley and enjoy.

Chicken livers peri-peri
Serves 8

I love organ meats and these chicken livers peri-peri deliver. Chicken livers are a cheap form of protein and those of us living in South Africa recognize the Portuguese community that introduced us to peri-peri. Nando's our own global brand, which emanates from South Africa, has made peri-peri chicken their legendary trademark. One of the early Paleo adopters, Mark Sisson writes that according to those in the know, liver is an excellent source of high quality protein; liver contains an abundance of vitamin A and several B vitamins; liver is an excellent source of folic acid and iron; liver is the number one food source of copper; and it contains CoQ10, which is important for cardiovascular function. More on Mark's website: www.marksdailyapple.com

1 onion, thinly sliced
½ tspn ground cumin
2 T free-range butter
2 cloves of garlic, crushed
½ tspn smoked paprika
500 g free range chicken livers (cleaned and trimmed)
100 ml cream
Sea salt
Portuguese rolls to serve

¼ tspn ground cloves
4 T Extra Virgin Olive oil
1 kg ripe tomatoes
1 tspn ground chilli flakes
Peri-peri sauce for extra heat
100 ml brandy
Flat leaf parsley
Freshly ground black pepper to taste

Melt 1T butter and 2T olive oil in a saucepan, add the sliced onion, the ground cloves and ground cumin and cook on a medium to low heat until golden brown. Set aside. Cut the tomatoes with a small X on the top, taking care not to cut too deep into the flesh. Bring a kettle of water to the boil and immerse the tomatoes, in a glass Pyrex bowl in the boiling water for 15 – 20 seconds. You will see the skin beginning to peel back. Immediately place the tomatoes in a bowl of ice water. Peel the skin from the tomatoes, then cut in half and half again. Remove the seeds, dice roughly and set aside. Using a pestle and mortar, create a paste from the ground chilli flakes, paprika and garlic.

Add 2T olive oil to a medium size saucepan, add the paste and fry for 1 minute. Add the chopped tomatoes and cook for a further 5 minutes. At this stage add your hot sauce, as spicy as you like. Allow the sauce to simmer on a low heat whilst you prepare the rolls and cook the livers. Cut a hollow in each Portuguese roll. These will act as a receptacle for your livers and the tops serve as lids. Toast under the grill or on the braai watching that the rolls don't burn. Add 1T butter to a large pan and heat. Add the chicken livers and cook on each side for a minute or two. Add the sliced caramelised onion and then the brandy. Be aware that the alcohol may catch alight, effectively flambéing the livers. To complete the dish, add the cream as well as the peri-peri tomato sauce, stirring to combine. Add the freshly chopped parsley. Spoon into the bread bowls, pop the lids onto the bread rolls and serve.

Coriander chicken with guacamole

Serves 8

Flavours of Mexico combine to produce a delicious chicken dish which your friends can assemble at table.

8 skinless, chicken breasts   8 flour tortillas, cut into wedges

Marinade
1 T each Extra Virgin olive oil and Tamari sauce   1 tspn each sesame oil and honey
1 T chopped coriander plus 2 sprigs
5 cm piece fresh ginger, peeled and grated on a Micro-plane

Guacamole
1 large ripe avocado, peeled   1 garlic clove, crushed
1 red chilli, deseeded and finely chopped   2 spring onions, finely sliced
Juice of 1 lime, plus ½ lime cut into wedges to serve
2 large tomatoes, peeled, deseeded and chopped

Wrap each chicken breast in cling film, place on a wooden chopping board and gently bash with rolling pin until 6 mm thick. In a bowl combine all marinade ingredients, add chicken and set aside for 15 minutes. For the guacamole, mash the avo with the lime juice, garlic, chilli, tomatoes, spring onions, coriander and season. Dry-fry the tortillas until crisp. Cook the chicken in a hot non-stick pan for 5 to 6 minutes on each side, slice and arrange on plates. Divide the guacamole between them and garnish with coriander. Serve with the tortillas and lime wedges.

Fricassée de poulet aux noix
Serves 8

This is the 2nd of my aunt Tante Mithé's dishes. This time the chicken is paired with walnuts and served on a cauliflower purée.

1 large free range chicken
200 g walnuts, of which 175 g to be finely crushed in a food processor

2 T organic butter	2 T Extra Virgin olive oil
1 T cornflour	3 onions, finely chopped
100 ml red wine	2 T tomato paste
1 cup homemade chicken stock	¼ tspn paprika
2 T parsley, chopped	Celery leaves, finely sliced

Cut the chicken into 8 pieces. Fry the onions in a pan with the oil and butter until lightly browned. Remove the cooked onions from the pan and set aside. Brown the chicken pieces in the remaining olive oil until golden. Return the onions to the pan and fry for 5 minutes on medium heat. Add the red wine, tomato paste and chicken stock to the pan. Add the crushed walnuts, cover the pan and allow the chicken to simmer for 45 minutes. Before serving, sprinkle the chicken fricassée with paprika, chopped parsley, sliced celery leaves and 25g walnuts.

Chicken tagine with preserved lemons
Serves 8

Foodie friend, Pam, gave us a large jar of preserved lemons one Christmas. The lemons were from Pam's garden and we used this gift to make a chicken tagine dish. The toasted spices in this dish combine to make this a delicious North African cuisine specialty.

Start this recipe the day before to allow the spice flavours to marinate the chicken pieces!

1 cinnamon stick
1 tspn cumin seeds
1 tspn chilli flakes
6 T Extra Virgin olive oil
2 tspn fresh ginger, chopped finely
3 bay leaves
1 large free range chicken, cut into 8 pieces
1 preserved lemon
1 cup of homemade chicken stock, using the carcass of the chicken

1 tspn whole black peppercorns
1 tspn hot paprika
¼ tspn whole cloves
5 clove of garlic, sliced
1 bunch fresh coriander, chopped
1 large pinch saffron
1 large onion, chopped
20 green olives, pitted

Put a non-stick pan onto medium heat and toast the cinnamon, peppercorns, cumin, paprika, chilli flakes and cloves until they start to smoke. Remove from the heat and grind in a spice grinder or a pestle and mortar. In a large glass bowl add the oil, ground spices, garlic, ginger, coriander, bay leaves and the saffron. Mix well. Add the 8 chicken pieces and rub the marinade all over the pieces of chicken. Cover the glass bowl with cling film and refrigerate overnight to allow the flavours to develop.

The next day, remove the chicken from the marinade and reserve the marinade. Pat the chicken dry and season the pieces with salt and pepper. Add 3T olive oil to a tagine or a large casserole dish, which you put onto medium heat. Lightly brown the chicken pieces all over. Add the onions and cook them until just starting to brown. Rinse the preserved lemon and cut it into strips and add the lemon pieces to the pan. At this stage add the reserved marinade, the green olives and the homemade chicken stock. Cover the tagine or casserole tightly and cook over medium low heat for 30 minutes or until the chicken pieces are cooked through. Remove the bay leaves and discard. Taste and adjust the seasoning accordingly. Place the chicken onto a warm serving dish and spoon the juices with the preserved lemon and olives over the chicken pieces. Serve this chicken tagine with the traditional couscous accompaniment.

Mauritian chicken and prawn curry
Serves 8

This is my version of a Mauritian chicken and prawn curry. I love the coconut milk flavour and combination of spices. The sambals, which I serve with the curry, are family favourites. I have included the sambal recipes in the book. If there is any leftover tomato chutney, Papa spreads it onto his bread at breakfast the next morning!

1 kg skinless, boneless chicken thighs
500 g shelled raw prawns (leave the tails on)
1 T coconut oil
4 T curry powder
1 tspn turmeric
2 tspn finely chopped garlic
2 tspn finely chopped ginger
5 sprigs thyme
5 sprigs parsley
32 sprigs coriander (keep 16 for garnish)
10 curry leaves
4 ripe tomatoes or 1 can tinned tomatoes, diced
1 large onion
200 ml coconut milk
salt and pepper

Add the chicken thighs, curry powder and turmeric to a large glass or ceramic dish. Chop the half the coriander, all the thyme and all the parsley. Add the curry leaves and chopped herbs to the chicken with half the oil, the chopped garlic and ginger, salt and pepper. Marinate for 30 minutes. Peel the onion, slice it finely and fry in remaining oil until golden. Add chicken and brown for 3 to 4 minutes. Add the diced tomatoes to the chicken. Cover and simmer for 15 minutes on a low heat until the sauce thickens. If necessary, add a little water.

Add the prawns and coconut milk, and cook for a further 5 minutes until the sauce thickens. Garnish the curry with the remaining coriander sprigs. Check the seasoning and serve hot with cauliflower rice and my Mauritian roasted tomato chutney, vegetable achards, sliced cucumber and freshly grated coconut and tamarind chutney and chopped green chilli.

Greek feta chicken

Serves 8

Easy, light and delicious served hot or cold. Also great to take on picnics, cut into bite-sized pieces.

200 ml double cream Greek yoghurt
2 cloves garlic, crushed
10 ml dried oregano
Maldon Sea Salt flakes and freshly ground black pepper to taste
8 free range chicken breast fillets, flattened slightly
1 round of crumbled organic Feta cheese

Mix all the ingredients, except the chicken and Feta, in a large ovenproof casserole dish. Add the chicken, cover the dish with cling film and refrigerate to allow chicken to marinate for 30 minutes. Preheat the grill inside your oven. Put the casserole dish under grill for 15 minutes watching carefully that the chicken does not burn. Remove the casserole dish and turn the chicken pieces over. Sprinkle the Feta cheese on top of the chicken pieces. Grill for a further 10 minutes or until cooked through. Serve with a big leafy salad or seared French green beans tossed with anchovies and chilli flakes.

Moroccan chicken

Serves 8

This is one of my favourite baked chicken dishes and I love the combination of dried fruit, olives and capers. The recipe must be prepared 24 hours in advance and proportions may be doubled if serving to a larger crowd.

8 chicken breast fillets
3 tspns dried oregano
¾ cup red wine vinegar
1½ cups pitted prunes, quartered
¾ cup green olives, pitted
4 bay leaves

4 cloves garlic, crushed
Salt and freshly ground black pepper
¾ cup virgin olive oil
¾ cup dried apricots (brightly coloured ones)
½ cup capers
1½ cups white wine

Spread the chicken fillets in a large Pyrex glass casserole. Combine the garlic, oregano, salt pepper, vinegar, oil, prunes, apricots, olives, capers and bay leaves and pour over the chicken. Cover and refrigerate overnight. The next day preheat the oven to 180°C. Pour the wine onto the marinated chicken and pop into the oven. Bake for 35 minutes or until the chicken is cooked. Serve the Moroccan chicken with couscous and garnish with coriander leaves.

Terrine de foie de volaille

Fills the Le Creuset terrine dish 28 cm or use a 1.1 litre terrine

This recipe was given to my parents, Monique and Maurice Labat by their good friend, Jacques Lenoir who ran a wonderful restaurant in Black River, Mauritius called La Bonne Chute. My thanks go to Nicole, Jacques' wife and her son, Benoît for giving me the permission to reproduce this recipe in English. Our family has been making this delicious chicken liver terrine for as long as I can remember. I have taken it to game reserves and on picnics!

750 g free range or organic chicken livers
300 ml full cream milk
2 small tins cream (155 g each)
300 g salted butter, organic
4 T Port or South African Cape Ruby
75 g spring onions, finely chopped
75 g Italian parsley, finely chopped
Freshly ground black pepper
1 ½ tspn sea salt

Start this recipe the day before.

With a small knife, trim the chicken livers of green stains. Remove the connective tissue. Put the cleaned livers into a medium sized glass Pyrex dish. Add the milk, half the spring onions and chopped parsley and a good sprinkling of black pepper. Cover the bowl with cling film and marinate the chicken livers overnight in the fridge.

After approximately 12 hours, strain the chicken livers and discard the milk. Leave the livers in the Pyrex bowl and add the Port, the remaining spring onions, parsley and freshly ground black pepper. Cook the livers in a double boiler by placing the Pyrex bowl onto a medium sized pot filled ¼ of the way with hot water. Bring the water to the boil, turn the heat down to low so that the water simmers. Gently cook the livers for 45 minutes, ensuring that the water in your pot does not evaporate. Once the livers have cooked, carefully remove the residue water that appears on top of the livers. Let the livers cool down and place them in the food processor. Process the livers to a paste. Add the cream, process further until well incorporated. Then add the butter to the livers. Process into a smooth creamy paste. Taste for seasoning.

Pour the chicken liver paste into a lined terrine dish. In order to preserve the terrine for up to two weeks, pour cooled clarified butter onto the chicken liver paste. Cover with the terrine lid or with aluminium foil and refrigerate for several hours to allow the flavours to develop. Unmould the terrine and serve with melba toast, homemade croutons using day old baguette or for a Paleo option toast slices of the seed loaf, sliced into triangles. Gherkins and caramelised onion marmalade works well with this terrine.

Duck

Duck confit rolls with chilli dressing

Serves 8

This impressive starter is colourful, crunchy and full of contrast. The dressing can be made in advance. Duck breasts may be a popular cut of this rich poultry bird, but I prefer using confit of duck legs. These can be bought ready-made or if you have the time, make the confit of duck legs yourself.

8 x 22 cm rice paper rounds
3 Lebanese cucumbers, sliced thinly lengthways
160 g shredded cooked duck
1 cup coriander leaves
1 cup basil leaves
micro herbs, to serve

Chilli dressing
60 ml fish sauce
60 ml rice wine vinegar
55 g brown sugar
125 ml water
2 cloves garlic, crushed
2 long red chillis, seeds removed and finely chopped
2 T lime juice

First make the chilli dressing. Place the fish sauce, vinegar, brown sugar, water and crushed garlic in a small saucepan over low heat, stirring until sugar has dissolved. Increase the heat to high, bring the dressing to the boil and cook for 8-10 minutes or until dressing has reduced and is sticky. Add the chilli and lime juice and stir to combine. Set aside to cool completely.

Soften a rice paper round in a large pie dish of warm water for 10 seconds. Place it on a clean bench top or large wooden chopping board sprinkled with a few drops of water and allow it to soften for a further 5-10 seconds. Place 5 cucumber slices, overlapping slightly, in the middle of the rice paper round. Top with 2 T shredded duck, a couple of coriander leaves and 2 basil leaves. Fold in both ends of the rice paper and roll to enclose the filling. Repeat with the remaining ingredients. Serve the duck rice paper rolls with the chilli dressing and micro herbs.

Duck leg confit with flageolet beans
Serves 8

Duck confit is a classic dish from the south west of France. Many homes in this region of France have a cellar. Jars of duck confit were prepared and stored in the cellar. Start this recipe a couple of days before serving.

8 large free range duck legs
60 g sea salt
2 T black peppercorns, crushed
8 garlic cloves, finely sliced
4 fresh bay leaves, sliced
8 sprigs of thyme, finely chopped
1,6 kg duck fat, melted

First one has to cure the duck legs. Lay the duck legs onto a baking tray, flesh-side upwards. Sprinkle the sea salt, the garlic, the crushed peppercorns, the sliced bay leaves and thyme evenly over the duck legs. Cover the baking tray with cling film and leave to marinate in the fridge overnight. The next day, rinse the marinade off the duck legs and pat them dry with a cloth.

To cook the duck legs, preheat your oven to 140°C. Put the duck legs into a large flameproof casserole and cover with the melted duck fat. Put the casserole onto a gentle heat bringing the fat to just below simmering. The temperature should reach 85°C. Ensure that there are no bubbles breaking the surface. Then transfer to the oven and cook uncovered for about 2 ½ hours until the duck legs are very tender. Leave to cool in the cooking fat in the refrigerator for 2 to 3 days and the flavour will further improve.

To serve the duck confit, take the legs out of the cooking fat very gently. Over a medium heat, in a dry frying pan, crisp and colour the duck legs on the skin side for 8 minutes. Flageolet beans are available in tins. Sauté some finely chopped shallots in duck fat until soft. Add a couple of sprigs of thyme. Add the tinned flageolet beans and heat through very gently. Divide the beans and some of their cooking liquid between 8 soup plates and top with the crispy duck legs. Drizzle over a little extra duckfat.

Fish
and
seafood

Mussels

From a very young age growing up on the South Coast of KwaZulu-Natal, my parents used to take us mussling at spring low tides. It was a real adventure. We packed our gardening gloves, mussel bags and permits and changed into our costumes. Once at the beach we'd wait until given the green light to head out onto the mussel-covered rocks, now exposed thanks to the low tide. We'd look for the largest mussels and twist and turn until they came away in our gloved hands. Then there was the job of scraping away the barnacles and bits of seaweed stuck to the mussel shells before being allowed to swim.

When little, Geneviève and I would spend Christmas holidays in Mauritius, where my grandfather Père Labat, would take us to Ilôt Sancho and there we'd pick bigornos or nerites clinging to the rocks. These would then be eaten in the fish soup for dinner. We have been hunter gatherers through the generations and learning the skill and knowledge at a tender age makes for an impressionable upbringing and is never forgotten. Special memories such as collecting mussels at low tide is not only a wonderful past-time, but you learn to appreciate nature's bounty.

Blue mussels (Mytilus galloprovincialis) belong to the Mytilidae family. Also called Blue mussels or Mediterranean mussel, this species is widely distributed around the world. This species was introduced onto the South African shores in the late 1970's. Within South Africa, the blue mussel stocks are said to be underfished at a rate, which is likely to maintain stock at healthy levels. Hand collection of blue mussels is reserved for recreational and subsistence fishers. Permit conditions stipulate that no more than 30 mussels per day are allowed by law to be collected in KwaZulu-Natal. Permits are compulsory and are valid for a period of one year from date of issue. The Annual Recreational Fishing Permit to quote its full name is available from our South African Post Offices at the cost of R94.00.

The Southern African Sustainable Seafood Initiative, www.sassi.mobi advises consumers what seafood can be consumed without fear of overfishing. The green list is the group from which people are encouraged to choose from, as it contains the best-managed, most sustainable choices available to consumers. Hand collection in South Africa targets all intertidal organisms, such as mussels, oysters and abalone. Oyster (S. margaritacea) is the only species that is commercially targeted. There are recreational permit conditions in place for these species too, which specify how many intertidal organisms are allowed to be collected per person, per day.

Mussels in verjuice

Serves 8

Verjuice is the unfermented juice blended from green harvested grapes. Its name in French means 'green juice'.

100 ml olive oil
5 cloves garlic, chopped
500 ml Verjuice
Juice & peel of 1 lemon
Handful basil, chopped
Sea salt

60 ml butter
3 onions, chopped
500 ml fish stock
2 kg mussels, cleaned
Handful Italian parsley, chopped
Freshly ground black pepper

Heat the olive oil and butter in a large pot. Sauté the garlic & onion until soft. Add the verjuice, fish stock, lemon juice and peel, and simmer for 5 minutes. Season well and toss in the mussels and herbs. Cover & simmer until all the mussels are open, about another 3-4 minutes. Discard all unopened mussels. Remove the beards from the mussels carefully without burning yourself. Taste for seasoning. Serve with a ciabatta loaf.

Mussels in laksa broth with lemongrass and bok choy

Serves 8

Lemongrass is very easy to grow and it's wonderful sharing cuttings with friends and family. Lemongrass loves sunlight and regular watering and it will reward you with lots lemony-scented stalks! Lemongrass makes a wonderful after dinner 'tisane' or infusion.

Start by making the laksa paste. This recipe will yield ¾ cup of paste. Most of these ingredients are available from Food Lover's Market throughout South Africa or at specialist Asian shops.

Laksa Paste

4 T lemongrass, finely minced
1 thumb-size piece of fresh ginger
½ cup coriander leaves and stems, chopped
1 T sesame oil
1 tspn shrimp paste
2 spring onions, sliced

5 cloves garlic
1 red chilli, sliced
2 T fish sauce
1 T Tamari
¼ cup freshly squeezed lime juice

Place all ingredients in a food processor. Blitz to create a fragrant laksa spice paste. If not using all the paste immediately, simply put the excess into a zip-lock bag and freeze.

Broth

60 fresh mussels, cleaned
1 onion, finely chopped
5 T laksa paste
2 cans coconut milk

1 T sesame oil
1 stalk lemongrass
1 cup dry white wine
1 bunch fresh coriander, washed, with stalks

Scrub the mussels well until clean. Set aside. Heat the oil in a large pot and gently fry onion until translucent. Add the laksa paste and fry for another two minutes. Add wine, mussels and lemongrass stalk, cover the pot with lid and allow to cook for about 5 minutes or until mussels have steamed open. *Remove the beards from the mussels carefully without burning yourself.* Remove the lemongrass stalk from the pot. Return the mussels to the pot in their shells, add the coconut milk and heat through. Check for seasoning. Garnish with fresh coriander and serve immediately in warmed bowls.

Anchovy omelette

Serves 2

We consume a lot of eggs on our Paleo diet and Francesco and I love anchovies. This omelette serves two and is a great Sunday evening staple if you're not hosting a dinner party! The photo above was taken on the 30th April 2011 and shows Ballycotton Harbour. Anne, Hetty, Johan and I would regularly cycle from Ballymaloe to Ballycotton and back after school food demos!

4 anchovy fillets, chopped
4 T filtered cold water
Sea salt and freshly ground black pepper
1 tspn Extra Virgin olive oil

4 large eggs, beaten
2 T chopped fresh herbs (parsley, chives, basil)
2 T butter

Mix together the anchovy fillets, eggs, water and chopped herbs. Heat the butter and oil in a frying pan. Pour the egg mixture into the hot pan. Keep lifting the edges to allow the liquid egg to run underneath. When eggs are set, fold the omelette over twice or just once. The inside should remain moist. Carefully season to taste with salt and pepper allowing for the saltiness of the anchovies. This omelette is wonderful served with ciabatta bread and marinated red and yellow peppers. The sweetness of the peppers offsets the saltiness of the anchovies beautifully.

Jinga masala

Serves 8

Thanks to best friend, Sharon for this recipe. I have served this at Bookclub evenings and at lunches and it never fails to impress. Jinga Masala goes well either with white Basmati rice or naan bread.

650g queen prawns, deveined and shelled, or substitute sliced chicken breasts

Tandoori Marinade
½ cup double cream Greek yoghurt
3 T sesame oil
1 tspn black mustard seeds
2 T freshly squeezed lime juice
3 cloves garlic
2 tspn chopped ginger
4 fresh small green chillies
1 T chopped mint
4 T chopped coriander
1 tspn cumin seeds roasted and ground
1 T garam masala
1 tspn sea salt

Place all the above tandoori marinade ingredients in a blender and blend to make a paste.

Sauce
4 T butter
2 medium onions chopped
½ cup full cream milk
30 ml tomato paste
2 fresh small green chillies, chopped
1 cup full fat cream

Fry onion in the butter for about 10 minutes over low heat without browning. Add the milk, tandoori marinade, tomato paste and chopped green chillies. Bring to the boil and cook for about 10 minutes stirring frequently. The mixture should be slightly reduced. Add the prawns and simmer for a further 5 minutes (if you are using sliced chicken breasts then simmer for 15 minutes). Stir in the cream and heat through for a further 5 minutes.

Prawn laksa
Serves 8

¼ quantity laksa paste
1 T fish sauce
1 T sesame oil
1 tray of bok choy, washed
1 bunch coriander, washed

750 ml organic chicken stock
40 medium prawns, deveined and shelled
1 can coconut cream
1 tray of shiitake mushrooms
4 spring onions, washed and sliced thinly

Put the stock and the fish sauce in a small saucepan and heat gently until very hot but not boiling. Set aside. Heat the oil in a large wok over low heat. Add the curry laksa paste and fry for about five minutes until fragrant. The oil will separate from the paste but do not worry. Add the hot stock to the wok and bring to the boil. Then reduce the heat and simmer for two minutes. Now add the coconut cream and cook for a further two minutes. Add the mushrooms and the prawns to the wok. Simmer for a few minutes then add the bok choy leaves. Taste for seasoning. Pour the prawn laksa into warmed bowls, scatter the coriander and spring onions over the soup and serve.

Steamed salmon fillets with orange and ginger butter
Serves 8

Mineola oranges are very easy to peel and pair beautifully with ginger to lift the taste of the salmon fillets

8 salmon fillets (or any other linefish)
2 tspn finely chopped fresh ginger
½ cup dry white wine
salt and freshly ground black pepper
aluminium foil cut into 8 pieces, about 30 cm square

4 mineola oranges, segmented
100 g butter, softened
lemon juice
sprigs of fresh dill

Preheat oven to 200°C. Season the fish fillets with salt, black pepper and lemon juice and set aside. Beat butter and ginger together until creamy. Grease foil squares with the butter and place the salmon fillets just below the centre of the foil. Divide the orange segments and dill into eight and arrange on top of each fish fillet. Sprinkle with white wine, fold over the aluminium foil and seal the edges well. Place on a baking sheet and cook in preheated oven for 15 minutes until the foil puffs up. Serve unopened with seasonal asparagus and oven roasted sweet potatoes.

Lamb

Barbecued lamb chops
Serves 8

South Africans are past masters at braaing meat. Braai verb South Africa: to grill meat, poultry or fish in the open air over the coals of a wood or charcoal fire. Origin from the Afrikaans 'braai' the verb meaning to grill and 'vleis' the noun meaning meat. In our Province of KwaZulu-Natal we also use the word 'shisa nyama' in IsiZulu to mean the same thing.
We have braai competitions, cookbooks dedicated to braaing and more recently a braai day which is celebrated on the 24th September, Heritage Day.

16 lamb loin chops
2 tspn mix of dried thyme, rosemary and oregano
8 small bay leaves, crushed
generous pinch paprika
finely grated rind and juice of 1 lemon
12 T Extra Virgin olive oil
Sea salt and freshly ground black pepper

Combine the herbs with the crushed bay leaves, paprika and lemon rind. Mix well, then rub the mixture onto the lamb loin chops. Lay the chops side by side in a shallow dish and pour over the lemon juice and olive oil. Season the chops, cover and leave to marinate for 3 hours, turning occasionally. Drain the chops, place onto the braai or barbecue and cook to your preference.

Cape Malay lamb curry
Serves 8

South Africa is a melting pot of cuisines. Our different cultures combine to give us excellent variety through choice local ingredients and traditional spicy dishes that have originated in far away lands. Fresh ginger is an essential component of this Cape Malay lamb curry.

1.2 kg boneless shoulder of lamb, cut into 5 cm pieces by your butcher
4 T Extra Virgin olive oil
4 large ripe tomatoes, chopped
4 T apricot jam
4 tspn mixed spice
4 tspn masala
2 T dried oregano
4 T dried golden sultanas
1 large knob fresh ginger, peeled and finely chopped

4 onions, chopped
4 T Mrs Balls fruit chutney
250 g packet dried apricots
4 tspn curry powder, medium strength
2 T mixed dried herbs
4 garlic cloves, crushed

Heat a heavy based pan and add the olive oil. Once the oil is hot add the chopped onions and turn the heat down to medium. Stir continuously and allow the onions to soften. Add the curry powder and stir well. Allow the curry powder to cook for several minutes stirring continuously ensuring it does not stick to the base of the pan. Add the masala and stir well for several minutes. Add the lamb pieces and brown until evenly coloured. Add the herbs, spices, garlic and ginger, salt and pepper to taste. Add the chopped tomatoes stirring to create a good sauce. Add the jam and the chutney, the sultanas and the dried apricots. Cook the curry on a low heat for approximately 1 hour. After this time, check whether the lamb is cooked through. Serve the curry with cauliflower rice and a selection of fresh sambals.

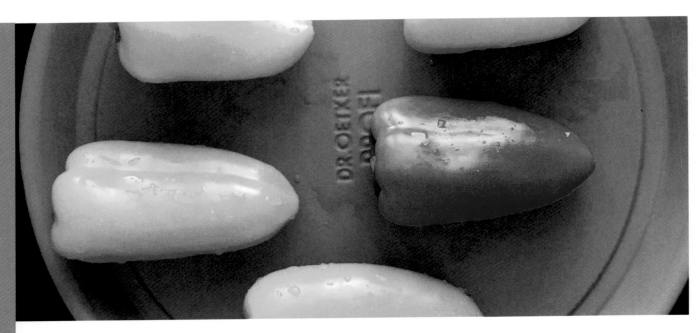

Lamb cutlets with peperonata

Serves 8

Lamb is one of my favourite meats. This dish has an Italian Mediterranean flavour thanks to the use of bright red and yellow peppers.

2 T thyme leaves
4 T extra virgin olive oil

4 garlic cloves, finely chopped
16 lamb cutlets

Peperonata

2 red peppers, quartered
4 T extra virgin olive oil
200 ml red wine vinegar
2 bay leaves
Sea salt

2 yellow peppers, quartered
2 onions, chopped
50 g castor sugar
2 sprigs thyme, finely chopped
Freshly ground black pepper

Combine the thyme, garlic and olive oil in a glass dish and season. Gently marinate the cutlets in the mixture by leaving the dish in the refrigerator for at least 1 hour. To make the peperonata, preheat the grill to high. Place the peppers, skin side up on a baking tray and drizzle with 2 tablespoon of extra virgin olive oil. Grill the peppers for about 20 minutes until charred. Transfer the peppers to a glass bowl, cover the bowl with cling film. Then peel the peppers and chop coarsely.

Heat the remaining olive oil in a pan over medium heat. Add the onion and cook stirring until soft. Add the red wine vinegar and the castor sugar to the pan, stirring to dissolve. Bring to the boil, add the herbs and peppers and simmer gently for a couple of minutes until most of the liquid has evaporated. Season the peperonata.

Preheat a chargrill pan on medium-high heat. Cook the lamb cutlets for 2 minutes on each side for medium rare. Serve with the peperonata.

Lamb loin, portobello mushrooms and lamb jus
Serves 8

Extra Virgin Olive Oil
8 x 200g boned lamb loins, trimmed of fat and sinews
freshly ground black pepper
400 g Portobello mushrooms, sliced

40 cloves of garlic, skin on
2 T sugar
100 g butter

To serve:
Sweet potato mash

Lamb jus (see page 96)

Preheat the oven to 230°C. Lightly oil a heavy based pan and place onto medium heat. When hot add the garlic cloves and stir until the cloves are coated with the oil. Transfer the pan to the oven and roast the garlic until cooked. The garlic cloves should have a crisp skin and be soft on the inside. Remove the garlic cloves from the oven and sprinkle the sugar onto the cloves. Return the pan to the oven and cook for a further 10 minutes until a crust forms on the garlic cloves. Set aside and keep warm.

Season the lamb loins with salt and pepper. Sear the lamb loins in a hot oiled pan. Transfer the lamb loins to the oven preheated to 220°C. Roast the lamb loins for approximately 5 minutes or longer if you prefer the lamb more well done. Remove the lamb from the oven. Carefully cover the lamb with aluminium foil and set aside to keep warm and to allow the lamb to rest.

Ensure your orange sweet potato mash is heated through and ready to serve. Heat the butter in a saucepan and sauté the sliced Portobello mushrooms until cooked. Season the mushrooms lightly. Heat the lamb sauce in a small saucepan and add a knob of butter to the sauce before serving. Slice the lamb loins across into thick slices and arrange on warmed individual plates. Add the mushrooms and garlic cloves and spoon the hot sauce over the lamb. Serve the lamb with the orange sweet potato mash.

Lamb jus

Serves 8

2kg chopped lamb bones with trimmings from your Butcher
50 g butter
1 celery stalk, finely chopped
1 large onion chopped
2 leeks, carefully washed and chopped
1 large carrot, chopped
2 litres filtered water
12 whole black peppercorns
Sea salt

Melt the butter in a large pot and add the vegetables. Sweat the vegetables gently. Add the bones and trimmings and brown lightly. Add the water, peppercorns and a little sea salt. Bring to the boil, then simmer uncovered for 1 hour. Strain the lamb stock through a fine sieve and return to the pan. Reduce the stock further by half. To use in the Lamb Loin recipe, reheat the sauce gently in a small saucepan and add a knob of butter to the sauce before pouring onto the lamb.

Ostrich

Baked aubergines with ostrich mince

Serves 8

Aubergine or melanzane as it is known in Italian is a big favourite in our home. This versatile vegetable is essential to Italian cuisine. Here the dish is prepared and baked with one of our favourite South African ingredients, ostrich. Years ago we were introduced to ostrich meat whilst staying at Thendele in the Drakensberg with good friends, Anne and Graeme. The same evening we sampled the braaied ostrich steak, a curious visitor came to the chalet. It was a large spotted genet cat!

4 aubergines
6 T Extra Virgin olive oil
2 garlic cloves, minced
1 onion, finely chopped
1 carrot, peeled and diced
1 celery stick, finely sliced
500 g ostrich mince
1 can organic chopped tomatoes
3 T pine nuts
3 T capers
2 tspn dried oregano
3 T freshly grated Parmigiano Reggiano
2 T raisins soaked in 50 ml rum
1 red pepper, sliced into strips

Cut the aubergines in half lengthways. Gently scoop out the aubergine flesh very carefully using a sharp knife. Ensure that you leave a thin layer of the aubergine flesh inside the skin. Chop the aubergine flesh and put it into a colander. Sprinkle the aubergine with salt and mix well. Allow to drain for approximately 30 minutes. Preheat the oven to 180°C. Heat 3 tablespoons olive oil in a large pan. Add the garlic, onion, carrot and celery and sauté over low heat until soft. Add the ostrich mince and cook for about 10 minutes stirring frequently.

Drain the aubergine flesh well and rinse to remove all the salt. Pat dry with kitchen paper and add to the ostrich mixture. Stir in the pine nuts, capers, oregano, Parmigiano Reggiano and rum-soaked raisins. Mix gently but thoroughly and taste in the event additional seasoning is required. Oil a large ovenproof baking dish with a couple of tablespoons of olive oil. Fill the aubergine shells with the ostrich mince filling. Top the filled shells with the red pepper strips and drizzle the top with a little olive oil. Put the aubergines into a baking dish, cover and bake for 30 minutes. Then remove the lid and continue cooking for a further 20 minutes. This dish works well served with a large green salad lightly dressed with walnut oil and white wine vinegar.

Ostrich chilli con carne

Serves 8

When we were young, my siblings and I enjoyed chilli con carne with beef mince, red haricot beans simmered in a Mauritian Créole tomato and braised onion sauce. The recipe was recently requested by my godmother, Sybille who remembers eating it on family visits to our farm on the South Coast! These days I make the chilli con carne using ostrich mince produced on farms in the Klein Karoo.

500 g ostrich mince
3 T Extra Virgin olive oil
1 T organic butter
3 onions, finely chopped
4 cloves of garlic, crushed
1 knob fresh ginger, peeled and crushed
8 sprigs parsley, chopped
4 sprigs thyme
1 celery stalk, finely sliced
1 large green chilli, finely sliced
2 cans organic chopped Italian tomatoes
2 T tomato paste
2 cans organic haricot beans
Sea salt
Freshly ground black pepper
1 T Tabasco® sauce

Melt the butter in a large pan and add the olive oil. Add the chopped onions and brown on medium heat. Add the crushed garlic and ginger and continue cooking on medium heat, stirring continuously. Add the ostrich mince and brown the mince all over. Add the chopped parsley, the thyme and the celery. Stir well. Now add the chopped tomatoes and the tomato paste. Season to taste. Add the Tabasco sauce and allow to simmer on low heat for 20 minutes. Drain the haricot beans and add to the pot. Heat through gently. Serve with Basmati rice and a fresh cucumber sambal.

Ostrich bobotie

Serves 8

This is my go-to dish when we host international visitors, and is a firm favourite with South Africans. Here I use ostrich mince.

60 g butter
1 T curry powder
2 slices homemade bread of your choice
1 kg ostrich mince
½ cup seedless raisins, soaked in rum or Cape Ruby
1 T apricot jam
Freshly ground black pepper
3 bay leaves

2 onions, finely chopped
1 tspn turmeric powder
1 cup milk
2 T lemon juice
1 T Mrs Balls® Chutney
2 tspn sea salt
3 eggs

Preheat the oven to 180°C. Melt the butter, add the onion and sauté until soft. It helps if you put a butter wrapper, butter side down on top of the onions on low heat for about 10 minutes, remembering to cover the pan. This retains the moisture in your pan. Remove the butter wrapper once the onions are soft. Add the curry and turmeric powder, stir well and cook for a couple of minutes further. Soak the bread slices in the milk. Add the mince to the softened onions and stir well. Squeeze the bread and reserve the milk. Add the bread to the mince mixture with the raisins, lemon juice, chutney, apricot jam, salt and pepper. Cook for a further 5 minutes on the stove. Transfer the meat mixture to a buttered shallow casserole dish. In a small bowl beat the reserved milk with the eggs and pour over the mince. Place the bay leaves on top. Bake for 45 minutes, then remove from the oven. Serve the ostrich bobotie hot with cauliflower rice.

Pasta

Fettuccine salad with baby spinach, prawns and avocado

Serves 8

This delicious salad is ideal served at lunch in hot weather. Many years ago Viv served this at our Catholic support group and generously shared the recipe with me.

300 g cooked fettuccine pasta, tossed with Extra Virgin olive oil
Sea salt and freshly ground black pepper to taste
10 fresh mint leaves, finely chopped
1 large bag organic baby spinach, carefully washed and spun dry
24 large peeled prawns, cooked in butter and white wine and cooled
1 stick celery, finely sliced
6 spring onions, finely sliced
3 T chives, finely snipped
3 avocados, sliced

Salad Dressing
2 T apple cider vinegar
4 T Extra Virgin olive oil
1 clove garlic, crushed

2 tspn Maille Dijon mustard
4 T avocado oil
20 fresh basil leaves

Cook the fettuccine pasta in plenty of boiling salted water until al dente. Drain and cool the pasta. Add the chopped mint and olive oil. Add the baby spinach and the cooled cooked prawns, celery, spring onions and chives. Toss the salad very gently with the vinaigrette and then add the avocado slices. The salad is ready to serve.

Due tagliatelle with figs and Parmigiano Reggiano

Serves 8

Francesco taught me how to prepare homemade pasta the Genovese way. Before the start of our Paleo food adventure, the quickest meal Francesco rustled up was 'due spaghetti' or two spaghetti. Spaghetti cooked al dente with extra virgin olive oil, sea salt and freshly ground black pepper was a meal on its own. Anchovies added to the spaghetti made the dish extra special. Tagliatelle pasta has a beautiful softness when combined with fresh figs. Add a touch of chilli flakes and some finely grated lemon zest and it feels as though you're orbiting in a gourmet food galaxy!

8 fresh figs, washed and dried delicately
1 tspn chilli flakes
Juice of 1 lemon
150 ml fresh cream, gently heated

3 T Extra Virgin olive oil
zest of 2 lemons, using a micro-plane
100 g Parmigiano Reggiano cheese, shaved
400 g egg tagliatelle pasta

Start by preparing the figs first. Cut each fig into 4 pieces. Grate the lemon rind using a Micro-plane and squeeze the juice of one lemon into a separate bowl. Slice the Parmigiano Reggiano onto a small plate. Bring a large pan of salted water to the boil. Add the egg tagliatelle and cook until al dente. Heat a large frying pan and add the olive oil. When the oil is very hot, carefully add the fig pieces to the frying pan. Turn the figs frequently whilst they caramelize. The process should not take more than 3 minutes. Add the chilli flakes to the frying pan and remove from the heat. Drain the tagliatelle pasta and place in a warmed dish. Gently warm the cream. Add the lemon zest and lemon juice to the cream and pour over the tagliatelle. Add the caramelized figs and shavings of Parmigiano Reggiano and serve.

Pork

Braised pork belly

Serves 8

Pork belly was a very underrated cut of meat and has made an excellent comeback, thanks to many chefs and cooking schools such as *Ballymaloe* encouraging the complete use of the animal from nose to tail.

2 deboned pork bellies, approximately 1 kg each
2 onions, chopped
2 celery sticks, sliced
150 ml sherry vinegar
1.5 litres organic chicken stock
20 coriander seeds

8 T Extra Virgin olive oil
2 leeks, sliced
8 garlic cloves, peeled
300 ml Tamari sauce
6 star anise
10 whole black peppercorns

Preheat the oven to 170°C. Heat a large flameproof cast iron dish capable of containing both pork bellies until very hot. Add 4 tablespoons of olive oil and brown the pork bellies all over until caramelized. Remove the pork bellies from the cast iron dish and place onto a plate. Add the rest of the olive oil and sauté the vegetables and the garlic for approximately 5 minutes. Deglaze with the sherry vinegar and cook until it has reduced by half. Put the pork bellies back into the cast iron dish onto the vegetables. Pour in the Tamari sauce and the organic chicken stock. Add the spices and bring to the boil. Place the cast iron dish into the preheated oven at 170°C and cook for 3 hours, basting the pork bellies with the stock juices at 30 minute intervals. The meat should be very tender and should offer little resistance when pushing a metal skewer into the centre of the pork bellies. Lift the pork bellies out of the cast iron dish and place onto a warmed plate. Remove the string from the pork bellies and cut into thick slices. Serve the pork with the pieces of carrots, onions, leeks and celery as well as seasonal green asparagus or crunchy green beans.

Jellied ham

Serves 8

I love discovering food styles and wines of France where each region is fiercely proud of their produce. On my first trip to the Continent with my parents, in the little village of Panthier, we had the privilege of being hosted by Maryvonne and Jean-Jacques who were fine gourmets. Upon our arrival for lunch, we were served *un jambon persillé* or jellied ham with parsley. Here is my version, which makes for a great picnic lunch served with Maille Dijon mustard and seed loaf!

Begin the recipe the day before.

6 gelatine leaves
900 g thickly sliced leg ham, chopped
4 T capers, rinsed and drained

3 cups organic chicken stock
15 cocktail gherkins, chopped
½ cup chopped flat-leaf parsley

To serve:

Maille Dijon mustard

Seed loaf

Soak the gelatine in cold water for about 8 minutes to soften. Place the chicken stock in a saucepan over medium heat and bring to the boil. Squeeze any excess from the gelatine and add it to the stock. Stir gently until the gelatine has dissolved. Set aside to cool.

Combine the ham, gherkins, capers and parsley in a bowl and season. Pack the mixture into 8 one cup (250 ml) ramekins and pour over the cooled stock. Cover with cling film and refrigerate overnight to set. The next day when ready to serve, briefly dip the base of each ramekin in hot water, then invert the jellied hams onto the serving plates. Serve with seed loaf and mustard.

Pork fillets with apple, prune and walnut
Serves 8—10

This is a very elegant dish, which can be made in advance. It's very practical when entertaining.

1 T lemon verbena leaves
250 g stoned prunes
Sea salt
450 g pork sausage meat
6 juniper berries, crushed
2 T chopped parsley
1 apple cored and diced
100 g butter
½ T honey

300 ml boiling water
4 large pork fillets
Freshly ground black pepper
1 clove garlic, crushed
1 T chopped chives
2 T dry white wine
55 g walnut halves
2 T avocado oil

Place the lemon verbena leaves in a Pyrex bowl. Pour over the boiling water and leave to infuse for 10 minutes. Strain the lemon verbena liquid over the prunes. Cover with cling film and leave for 3 hours.

Split each pork fillet lengthways taking care not to cut right through the fillets. Open each fillet and flatten to a thickness of about 1 cm with a mallet. Season with sea salt and freshly ground black pepper.

Make the stuffing by mixing the pork sausage meat, garlic, juniper berries, chives, parsley, wine and apple. Season lightly. To test for seasoning in a stuffing that contains raw meat, simply fry off a teaspoonful of the stuffing in a little oil until just firm, then taste it and adjust the seasoning accordingly.

Arrange the prunes and walnuts alternately over 3 of the fillets. Divide the stuffing between the fillets, spreading in an even layer. Stack on top of each other. Place remaining fillet on top. Tie layers with string in 6 places. Wrap the meat in oiled aluminium foil and chill for 24 hours to allow the flavours to develop.

The next day, preheat the oven to 190°C. Melt the butter, oil, honey and wine in a pan on top of the stove. Remove the meat from the aluminium foil. Place the meat on a rack in a roasting pan, adding a little water to the pan. Roast for an hour, or until cooked through, basting occasionally with the butter mixture. Remove from the oven, cool, wrap in aluminium foil and chill in the refrigerator until ready to serve. If you choose to serve the pork fillets hot, use the remaining sauce in the roasting pan as your gravy.

122

Vegetables

Cauliflower coriander rice
Serves 8

In order to keep our carbohydrate intake to a minimum, Francesco and I have experimented with substitutes for rice and pasta. Our Italian and French-Mauritian heritage used to mean eating homemade pasta prepared with '00' wheat flour and Créole dishes served with white Basmati rice as staples. Nowadays we use a variety of vegetables such as baby marrow, butternut and cauliflower to replace pasta and rice. This rice replacement pairs well with Indian and Mexican dishes too!

1 large head cauliflower
¼ cup fresh coriander, chopped

1 T butter or coconut oil
Sea salt and black pepper

Remove the outer leaves and stem from the cauliflower and chop it into large chunks. Shred the cauliflower using a box grater or food processor. In a large pan over medium heat, melt the butter or coconut oil and place the shredded cauliflower into the pan. Season with sea salt and freshly ground black pepper. Sauté for 5 minutes or until cauliflower becomes translucent, stirring gently to ensure it cooks through. Place the cooked cauliflower into a serving bowl. Toss with the chopped coriander before serving.

Cauliflower purée

Serves 8

This dish is one of my favourite accompaniments to meat.

1 large head cauliflower
4 T butter
4 T organic fresh cream, gently heated
Butter
Sea salt to taste
Freshly ground black pepper

Chop the cauliflower into approximately 6cm pieces. Steam the cauliflower until it is fork-tender and place it in a food processor. Add the butter and the hot cream and purée until smooth and creamy. Season to taste. If you don't have a food processor, mash the cauliflower by hand with a potato masher. When ready to serve, put a large spoonful onto the plate, pop a small pat of butter on top of the cauliflower purée and add a good grind of black pepper.

Gruyère sweet potato gratin
Serves 8

2 T unsalted butter
1 cup full cream milk
1 kg sweet potatoes, peeled and thinly sliced
½ cup grated Gruyère cheese
Sea salt and freshly ground black pepper

Preheat the oven to 170°C. Butter an ovenproof cast iron casserole dish. Add the milk, season with salt and pepper to taste. Heat through and when hot, remove. Add the sweet potatoes arranged in overlapping circles and sprinkle with cheese. Simmer on top of the stove for 15 minutes then transfer to the oven and bake until potatoes are tender and the top is golden brown. This dish is delicious with beef or it can be layered with strips of ham for a light supper dish.

Cheddar cheese and leek ramekins

Serves 8

This is a simple savoury bake, which cooks quickly in individual ramekins. Fresh breadcrumbs make the texture more substantial.

1 kg leeks, washed thoroughly and white parts finely sliced
2 T Extra Virgin olive oil
8 large eggs, beaten
250 g Mature cheddar cheese
Sea salt and freshly ground black pepper
Fresh Italian parsley to garnish

2 cloves garlic, crushed
100 g fresh breadcrumbs
2 tspn dried tarragon
Butter for greasing

Preheat the oven to 200°C. Heat the oil and gently cook the leeks and garlic for 10 minutes. In a separate bowl, mix together the eggs, breadcrumbs, cheese and tarragon. Then add the cooked leeks and season the mixture well. Grease 8 large (150ml) ramekins thoroughly with butter. Spoon in the leek mixture and bake for 15 minutes. Leave to stand for a couple of minutes, then run a knife round the edge of the ramekin and turn out. Serve immediately garnished with parsley and accompanied by a green salad.

Hot marinated mushrooms

Serves 8

This recipe is easy to prepare and is a tasty way of cooking mushrooms.

50 g butter
800 g button mushrooms

Dressing
2 lemons, 4 T juice and 2 tspn grated lemon rind
2 tspn clear honey
2 tspn Maille Dijon mustard
2 tspn dried thyme
Sea salt and freshly ground black pepper

Gently melt the butter, then add the mushrooms and cook for 5 minutes. Mix the dressing ingredients together. Remove the pan from the heat and pour in the dressing. Serve hot.

Mushroom scrambled eggs

Serves 8

8 large mushrooms
8 T butter
1 tspn dried marjoram
2 tspn Dijon mustard
Sea salt and freshly ground black pepper
8 large free-range eggs
4 T cream
2 tspn chopped chives

Carefully wipe each mushroom using a damp cloth or mushroom brush. Remove the stems. Heat 4 tablespoons butter in a saucepan, add the marjoram, mustard and seasoning to taste. Grill the mushrooms in the oven until almost soft. Remove, set aside and keep hot. Melt remaining butter in a saucepan. Whisk the eggs lightly with cream, seasoning and chives. Scramble the eggs in a small heavy-based saucepan using a wooden spoon. Stir until creamy, remove and pile on mushrooms and serve immediately.

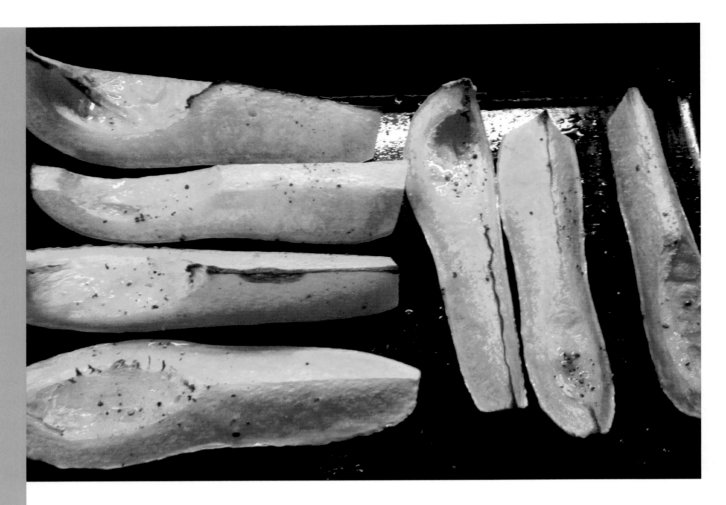

Roasted butternut wedges

Serves 8

These wedges are a delicious accompaniment to roast meats. You can also serve the butternut wedges cold, drizzled with Mauritian egg salad dressing alongside a green salad as a non-meat option.

1 large butternut weighing about 1.5 kg
Freshly ground black pepper
Fleur de Sel or Maldon salt flakes
Extra Virgin Olive oil for drizzling

Preheat the oven to 190°C. Rinse the whole butternut under tap water. Put the butternut onto a large wooden chopping board. Sharpen a large chopping knife. Very carefully slice the butternut in half. Chop each half in half again and again. You should have 8 long wedges of butternut. Place the unpeeled butternut wedges onto a large flat oven tray and drizzle the olive oil quite sparingly onto each slice. Season the butternut and pop the oven tray into the oven. Roast for 40-45 minutes. Test with a skewer to ensure the butternut is cooked through.

Sweet potato mash
Serves 8

1 kg orange flesh sweet potato
1 tspn sea salt
100 g butter, cubed

Peel the sweet potatoes and cut into large chunks. Pop the sweet potato into a thick-based pot and barely cover with water. Add the salt, cover and bring to the boil. Continue cooking for a further 10 minutes. Drain the sweet potatoes, mash lightly and add the cubed butter. Give the mash a good stir and keep warm until needed.

Dessert
and
ice-cream

Apple and cheddar cheese crumble
Serves 8

Some childhood memories never fade. Growing up on the South Coast, my sister Geneviève and I were best friends with Diana and Penelope. The apple crumble served at Scotia was delicious. Another treat reserved for Sunday evenings, were pancakes made by Diana's Dad. The pancakes were served with a sprinkling of cinnamon, brown sugar and freshly squeezed lemon juice. They were rolled up and devoured by the four of us in a matter of seconds!

6 large Granny Smith apples
½ tspn cinnamon
½ cup maple syrup or honey
½ cup cake flour
½ cup cheddar cheese, grated

1 T freshly squeezed lemon juice
½ tspn freshly grated nutmeg
3 T sugar
6 T butter, cubed
Pinch of salt

Preheat the oven to 180°C. Peel and slice the Granny Smith apples into a buttered oven-proof dish measuring 25 cm x 15 cm. Sprinkle the sliced apples with the lemon juice, cinnamon and nutmeg. Pour the maple syrup or honey over the apples. In a separate bowl mix the flour, sugar and butter until the mixture resembles breadcrumbs. Add the grated cheddar cheese and sprinkle this onto the apple mixture. Bake the crumble for 35 minutes. Serve with cream or homemade vanilla ice-cream.

Apple omelette
Serves 2

The French make excellent use of eggs especially in desserts. This delicious apple omelette is a beautiful comforting dessert, which requires last minute preparation. For that reason this recipe serves two!

2 large Granny Smith apples
1 T sugar
2 T double thick cream
3 large free range eggs, separated
Icing sugar for dredging

2 ½ T butter
1 T rum or brandy
Ground cinnamon
Pinch of sea salt

Peel the apples and slice very thinly. Cook the apple slices very gently in the butter for 10 minutes or until tender, turning often. Add the alcohol, cream and a sprinkling of cinnamon. Set aside. Beat the egg whites with salt until stiff. Whisk the egg yolks using the same beaters. Fold the egg yolks and whites together. Cook in the remaining butter until golden underneath. Slide under a heated grill for a minute or two until puffed up and just set. Top the omelette with the hot, cooked apple mixture. Sprinkle with sifted icing sugar and serve immediately. If you wish, flame some rum or brandy and pour over the omelette!

Apples with sweet verjuice butter
Serves 8

8 Golden Delicious apples, halved
200 g butter chopped
½ cup Demerara sugar, unrefined sugar blended with aromatic treacle syrup

Sweet Verjuice Butter
250 g unsalted butter
Juice & peel of 2 oranges
1 cup verjuice

Juice of 1 lemon
1 cup sugar

Preheat the oven to 180°C. Place the apples in an ovenproof dish, cut side up, and top with butter & sugar. Bake basting frequently until the apples are soft, 45 minutes. To make the verjuice butter, melt the butter in the pan set over low-medium heat until it smells nutty and is brown. Remove from the heat and add the lemon juice, orange juice, peel and sugar. Return to the heat and stir until the sugar dissolves. Pour in the verjuice and stir until the sauce thickens slightly, about 5 minutes. Serve poured over the apples with whipped cream, mascarpone or ice-cream.

Fruit parcels

Serves 8

Use the practical list of seasonal fruit in the front of this book to create your own fruit parcel combinations.

4 bananas
4 ripe nectarines
5 plums
juice of 4 oranges
4 T brown sugar

30 strawberries
5 apricots
4 T rum
1 tspn ground cinnamon
¼ cup flaked toasted almonds

Greek full cream yoghurt or double thick cream for serving

Heat the oven to 200°C. Peel and slice the bananas. Wash and hull the strawberries. Halve and stone the nectarines, plums and apricots. Cut into wedges. Divide the fruit equally between 8 pieces of heavy aluminium foil. Mix the rum, orange juice, cinnamon and sugar and drizzle over the fruit parcels. Crumple the foil to seal the parcels, leaving room for the air to circulate. Bake for 15 minutes. Open the parcels, sprinkle with toasted flaked almonds. Serve with Greek yoghurt or double thick cream.

Avocado coconut vanilla bean ice-cream
Serves 8

We are fortunate to have many avocado varieties in South Africa, namely Fuerte, Pinkerton, Hass, Reed, Edranol and Ryan. Our avocados are in season from March through to November. Westfalia, one the largest avocado producers in South Africa, grow conventional as well as organic avocados and their orchards are situated mainly in the Modjadjiskloof area in the Limpopo Province and in Howick, KwaZulu-Natal province. The Limpopo Province is in the north of South Africa on the Drakensberg escarpment while the KwaZulu-Natal Province is situated in the south east of the country on the Indian Ocean coast line. Westfalia's range of avocado products include avocado oil, guacamole and whole avocados.

This recipe is delicious and requires no added sugar. The creaminess of the coconut comes from the first pressings of the coconut flesh. The canned variety does include some added sugar so check the label under typical nutritional information. Homemade coconut milk can be substituted for the canned coconut cream. I have included the recipe below.

Check the ice-cream manufacturer's instructions before starting on this recipe. My Krups ice-cream maker bowl has to be placed in the freezer the day before I make the ice-cream. Once the ice-cream has almost set in the ice-cream maker, pour the ice-cream into another container and return to the freezer.

2 ripe Hass avocados
2 x 400 ml (cans) coconut cream or the homemade variety below
1 vanilla bean, sliced in half lengthways and scraped into the coconut cream
2 T light rum (optional)
1 lime, freshly squeezed

Halve the avocados and remove the pit. Scoop out the flesh and put it in a blender or the bowl of a food processor. Add the coconut cream, vanilla bean, rum and lime juice and process until completely smooth. Chill the mixture thoroughly in the refrigerator.

Once chilled, pour into your ice-cream maker and churn according to the manufacturer's instructions. Once the ice-cream has set in the ice-cream maker, pour the ice-cream into another container and return to the freezer. Once frozen, remove the ice-cream from the freezer and thaw slightly before serving.

Raspberry coulis

A berry coulis is delicious served with the avocado coconut and vanilla bean ice-cream. A quick tip – make the sugar syrup first and then continue with the raspberry coulis.

100 g castor sugar
15 g liquid glucose
100 ml water

Combine the castor sugar, liquid glucose and the water in a saucepan. Bring slowly to the boil over low heat. Stir continuously with a wooden spoon to dissolve the castor sugar. Boil for 3 minutes. Pour the syrup into a glass Pyrex jug. The sugar syrup will also keep in an airtight container in the refrigerator for 2 weeks.

500 g ripe raspberries
175 ml sugar syrup
½ lemon, juiced

Put the raspberries, the sugar syrup and the freshly squeezed lemon juice into a blender. Process until smooth, approximately 1 minute. Pass the coulis through a muslin lined strainer or a fine-meshed conical sieve. Refrigerate until needed.

Homemade coconut milk

Cooking is very therapeutic for me. I take great pleasure in producing food from scratch, enjoying each step of the handmade process.

227 g pack of shredded coconut
4 cups of hot water, not boiling

Place the coconut and hot water in a blender for about 45 seconds. Line a strainer with 2 layers of muslin or use a nut milk bag. Pour the contents of the blender through the strainer into a large bowl. Bring the edges of the muslin together. Squeeze out the remainder of the coconut milk. Refrigerate the coconut milk and use within 2 days. I freeze the homemade coconut milk in zip lock bags. Remember to leave some space at the top of the bag before sealing it and popping the bag into the freezer.

Coconut cream
Makes 8

Living in a tropical climate is wonderful. An abundance of fruit can be used to supplement ingredients in recipes originally produced in the Northern Hemisphere.

1 x 400 ml can coconut milk
250 ml fresh cream
150 g brown sugar
1 tspn Vanilla extract
5 free range eggs

Preheat the oven to 160°C. In a medium sized saucepan heat the coconut milk, the cream and the sugar until the sugar dissolves. Remove from the heat and add the vanilla extract. In a separate bowl beat the eggs lightly. Pour the hot cream mixture onto the lightly beaten eggs and whisk well. Strain the mixture into a Pyrex jug and then pour into 8 ramekins. Put the ramekins into an oven tray or large roasting dish and half fill the tray or dish with hot water. Bake in the oven for 30 minutes. Remove from the oven and allow the coconut creams to cool. Refrigerate the ramekins and serve once cold.

Basil yoghurt ice-cream with chocolate almond cake and fresh strawberries

Serves 8

To make this delicious dessert combination, add some freshly sliced seasonal strawberries to the dessert plate and drizzle with balsamic vinegar.

Basil Yoghurt Ice-cream
- 80 g or 1 large bunch fresh basil
- 500 g castor sugar
- 250 g mascarpone cheese
- 1 kg double cream Greek yoghurt

Place the basil leaves and castor sugar in a food processor and pulse until the mixture forms a coarse powder. Add the mascarpone cheese and the Greek yoghurt, then pulse to combine. Churn the mixture in an ice-cream machine according to the manufacturer's instructions, then freeze until firm. Prepare 1 scoop per person in advance of your dinner party by scooping the ice-cream onto a cling film covered plastic chopping board. Pop the scoops of ice-cream back into the freezer until needed.

Chocolate Almond Cake
- 100 g 70% Lindt dark chocolate, chopped into small pieces
- 100 g Lindt milk chocolate, chopped into small pieces
- 200 g unsalted butter, cubed
- 4 large free-range eggs
- 200 g castor sugar
- 200 g ground almonds
- 50 g cocoa powder
- 1 tspn baking powder

Heat the oven to 190°C. Lightly grease and line a 23cm round, spring-clip cake tin. Melt the chocolate in a heatproof bowl set over a pan of barely simmering water. Add the cubed butter a few cubes at a time and stir gently until melted. Set aside to cool for 20 minutes. In a large bowl whisk the eggs and the castor sugar until pale and fluffy, then gently fold in the cooled chocolate mixture. Mix the ground almonds, cocoa powder and baking powder together in a bowl and then gently fold this into the chocolate mixture. Be careful not to knock too much air out of the whisked eggs. Pour into the prepared tin and bake in the middle of the oven for 20-25 minutes until just set. Leave to cool in the tin. Transfer the cake to a serving plate.

To serve: Place a slice of the Chocolate Almond cake onto a chilled dessert plate and add a scoop of Basil Yoghurt ice-cream. Dust the slice of cake with a little icing sugar and place some sliced strawberries next to the cake. Drizzle some balsamic vinegar onto the strawberries to serve. South African Cape Ruby pairs well with this dessert!

Baked apples with rum raisins and coconut shavings

Serves 2

A glass jar filled with sundried raisins, topped with rum is a great dessert staple to store in your refrigerator. It will keep for weeks and can be sprinkled onto ice-cream or over hot bread and butter puddings. Here the rum raisins are used in the baked apple dessert.

8 large Honey Crunch apples grown in South Africa
100 g butter
12 almonds, chopped into slivers
1 tspn cinnamon

lemon juice
2 T raisins that have soaked in rum
2 T coconut shavings
250 ml Double thick cream

Preheat your oven to 180°C. Core the apples and score the skin around the fattest part of the apple. Mix the butter with the raisins, almonds, coconut and cinnamon. Drizzle the lemon juice into the cored apples and then spoon the butter mixture into the apples. Stand the apples in an ovenproof baking dish. Pop the dish into the hot oven and bake for 45 minutes. Carefully put the baked apples onto the dessert plates, make quenelles of the Double thick cream and drizzle some extra rum soaked raisins onto the dessert plate.

Guava ice-cream, French meringue and crème à la vanille

Serves 12

On Friday evening, 31st August 2012 we celebrated a special dinner at Simbithi Country Estate. We had received a telephone call a week earlier from good friends, Sharon and Trevor. They had been given a leg of impala and asked if I would cook the venison and then serve it at dinner at Wendy and Peter's home on the North Coast. This was the opportunity to put some wild game cooking into practice. Caul and spek, the Afrikaans word for bacon was obtained thanks to a visit to our local butcher. The leg of impala was delivered to our home weighing 4.8 kgs! Undaunted, a large new oven tray was secured and the venison was marinated in a bottle of Stellenzicht Pinotage 2008 for 2 days and then slowly roasted at 150°C for 5 hours. That evening, for starters Antonella had made delicious Camembert and Onion marmalade puff pastry wedges. Sharon had prepared a large tray of roasted vegetables and a delicious green salad to accompany the roast impala. Three different South African red wines were served with the roast leg of impala - the Stellenzicht Pinotage 2008, the Kloovenburg Shiraz 2008 and an Uva Mira Syrah. To round off the evening we served guava ice-cream, French meringue and crème à la vanille dessert. *Please note that all the components of this recipe serve 12.*

Guava Ice-cream

1 ½ cups water
1 whole star anise
8 ripe guavas
1 thumb-sized strip of fresh lemon zest, pith removed

1 cup white sugar
4 cm quill of cinnamon
2 tspn fresh lemon juice
¼ cup cream

Put the water, sugar, star anise, cinnamon and lemon zest into a saucepan and bring slowly to the boil, stirring occasionally. Simmer for 10 minutes, or until the sugar syrup is quite clear. Set aside to cool completely, then place in the fridge for an hour or two until cold. Top and tail the guavas, but do not peel. Cut into chunks and place in a food processor fitted with a metal blade. Whizz to a rough purée. Tip the purée into a sieve set over a large bowl and, using the back of a soup ladle, press vigorously down on the pulp, straining off the liquid. Discard the pulp and seeds that remain in the strainer. Strain the chilled sugar syrup into the bowl containing the strained guava and discard the spices and lemon peel. Add the lemon juice and cream, and stir well to combine. Place the mixture in the bowl of an ice-cream machine and churn until done.

French Meringue

5 egg whites
150 g icing sugar

150 g castor sugar

Preheat the oven to 100°C. Line a baking sheet with a Silpat mat. Beat the egg whites in a clean bowl, using an electric mixer until softly peaking. Still whisking, add the castor sugar and continue whisking until the mixture forms firm peaks. Add the icing sugar and continue to beat until the meringue forms stiff peaks and is smooth and shiny. This will take approximately 7 minutes. Shape the meringues into quenelles onto the Silpat mat. Place in the oven and bake for 1 hour and 50 minutes. Leave the meringues to cool and then transfer to a wire rack.

Crème à la Vanille

If you enjoy making custard and other cooked desserts, reserve a saucepan just for dessert items especially to retain the delicate taste of crème à la vanille.

5 large egg yolks
4 T white sugar
1 dessertspoon cornflour
1 vanilla bean
3 cups full cream milk

Rinse a thick-based saucepan with cold water. Pour the milk into the saucepan. Add half the vanilla bean and its seeds to the milk. Heat until almost boiling. Put the egg yolks and sugar in a bowl and beat using an electric beater until the mixture thickens and becomes pale yellow. Add the cornflour and the other half of the vanilla bean including its seeds to the egg mixture. Beat once more. Slowly pour the hot milk onto the egg mixture stirring continuously. Pour the milk mixture back into the thick base saucepan. Turn the heat to medium. Stir continuously using a wooden spoon reserved only for desserts until the custard thickens. Remove from the heat, allow to cool and refrigerate until needed.

To assemble: gently pour the vanilla custard into each dessert plate. Add a meringue to the plate and top the meringue with a scoop of guava ice cream.

Baked vanilla cheesecake with fresh berries

Serves 8

It's fun to surprise friends with a home-baked treat when they have helped you create a special profile on social media and on your website — just ask Alma and Karen!

40 g almond flour
45 g castor sugar
330 g mascarpone cheese, at room temp
4 large eggs, organic or free range, at room temp, slightly beaten
240 g castor sugar
1 T grated lime rind
1 ½ T cornflour
Fresh strawberries, raspberries, gooseberries or blueberries to serve and Icing sugar for dusting.

110 g cake flour
90 g unsalted butter, cubed
500 g ricotta cheese, at room temp
60 ml lime juice, freshly squeezed
½ tspn vanilla extract
1 ½ T water

Start by making the cheesecake base first so that the tin and the base are cool when you pour the cream cheese mixture into the baking tin. First wrap the pan with aluminum foil on the bottom and up the sides very carefully. This is to place the baking tin in a water bath later.

Preheat oven to 150°C. Place the almond flour, cake flour, castor sugar and butter in a bowl and rub with your fingertips to form a rough dough. Using the back of a spoon, press the mixture into the base of a lightly greased 20cm spring-form tin lined with non-stick baking paper. Bake for 25-30 minutes or until light golden. Set aside and allow the baking tin and base to cool completely.

Place the mascarpone, ricotta, castor sugar, lime juice, grated rind and vanilla extract in a food processor and process until combined. Gently add the lightly beaten eggs and process until just combined. Mix the cornflour and water in a small bowl until smooth and add to the cheese mixture.

Place the baking pan in a large roasting pan. Fill the baking pan with cheesecake filling. Then, fill the roasting pan with about 3cms of hot water. I usually fill with water once placed in the oven to bake because it is hard to transfer a water-filled roasting pan with a cheesecake inside of it into the oven and not spill.

Bake for 45 minutes. The centre should still be slightly wobbly. Turn the oven off and allow the cheesecake to cool in the oven with the door closed for 1 hour. Sudden changes in temperature often cause cracking. Remove from the oven, allow to cool completely. Cover the cheesecake with cling film and refrigerate for 6-8 hours or preferably overnight.

Remove the cheesecake from the tin and top with strawberries, raspberries, gooseberries or blueberries. Dust with icing sugar to serve. The cheesecake will keep in the fridge, covered, for up to 3 days.

Chocolate terrine with fleur de sel caramel sauce

Serves 8

Black River, Mauritius, has the perfect climate for producing salt. Not just any salt, but fleur de sel. This salt is hand harvested from the salt pans at Mamie's family seaside farm, *Les Salines*. Sprinkle fleur de sel on both sweet and savoury dishes to extract maximum flavour.

200 g Lindt 70% Dark chocolate cocoa solids, broken into pieces
100 g icing sugar
175 g unsalted butter, softened
5 large eggs, separated
90g cocoa powder
a pinch of salt
200 ml pouring cream

Caramel
1 cup pouring cream
60 g butter, chopped
1 cup brown sugar
½ tspn sea salt flakes

Melt the chocolate in a heatproof bowl suspended over a saucepan of barely simmering water. Stir in the icing sugar, then the butter. Whisk in the egg yolks and the cocoa powder. Add a pinch of salt. Whisk the egg whites until soft peaks form. Whip the cream until thick and fold the egg whites and the cream into the mixture, ensuring they are well incorporated.

Sprinkle a little water inside the loaf tin. Line the loaf tin with clingfilm. Pour the mixture into the loaf tin and freeze overnight. Remove the terrine from the freezer about 15 minutes before slicing and serve with the Fleur de Sel Caramel Sauce.

To make the caramel, place the cream, butter and sugar in a saucepan over low heat and stir until the sugar is dissolved. Increase the heat to medium, bring to the boil, and cook for 5 minutes or until thickened. Allow to cool. Slice the terrine, drizzle over the caramel sauce and sprinkle with the sea salt flakes to serve.

Chocolate soufflés
Makes 8

These melting chocolate puddings are easier to make than ordinary soufflés. They are made ahead, but not cooked until required. Keep these unbaked chocolate soufflés in the fridge until you need them and remember to add a couple of minutes to the cooking time to compensate for the cold. The middle should still be saucy when they are ready.

200 g Lindt 70% Dark chocolate, chopped	6 large eggs
175 g sugar	125 g cake flour, sifted
150 g unsalted butter, cut into cubes plus	Extra butter for the ramekins

Heat the oven to 180°C. Butter 8 medium-sized ramekins. Melt the chocolate with the 150 g butter in a double boiler until melted. In a separate bowl, beat the eggs with the sugar until they are very light and fluffy. Then fold in the sifted flour. Gently fold in the chocolate mixture. Divide between the ramekins. Put in the fridge at this stage if you're making ahead. If baking immediately then bake for 8-12 minutes, the soufflés should rise and form a firm crust but you want them still to be slightly runny in the middle. To serve, put the hot ramekins onto a dessert plate and pass around a small milk jug with cream. You can also decorate the dessert plate with some fresh raspberries or strawberries.

Strawberry, balsamic and black pepper ice-cream

Makes 8

Forever remembered by Ali, Carin, Gwyn, Kim and Sheila as the dessert in the Facebook Challenge — night of the 28th Feb 2012!

2 cups fresh strawberries
½ cup castor sugar
2 T Balsamic Vinegar
2 tspn freshly ground black pepper
2 cups double cream
6 sheets of nori

Rinse, hull and slice the strawberries. Mix the sliced strawberries with castor sugar. Add Balsamic vinegar and freshly ground black pepper. Cover and allow to marinate in the fridge for 30 minutes. Blitz strawberries in the blender and fold in the double cream. Chill the mixture for one hour in the fridge and then freeze as per ice-cream maker's instructions. If you wish to serve the ice-cream in nori sheets, then soften the ice-cream a little and place the nori sheet onto a sushi mat, shiny side up. Gently spread the ice-cream at the top end of the nori sheet, about 5 cm wide, add a layer of sliced strawberries or fresh whole raspberries on top of the ice-cream in a single row. Gently roll the nori sheet using the mat to guide you. Seal the end of the nori sheet with your finger dipped in cold water. Wrap the nori ice-cream roll in cling film and freeze. Remove from the freezer 15 minutes before serving. Using a sharp knife, gently slice through the nori sheets, turn each slice sideways so you can see the strawberries in the centre. This is excellent served with the raspberry coulis on page 130.

Choux buns with crème pâtissière au chocolat

Makes approximately 40 choux buns

I reminded my niece Rachel that when we got a craze making choux à la crème in Hibberdene, we did not own a piping bag! Instead we used two small teaspoons to shape the choux pastry and it worked beautifully. You can easily adapt this recipe to make savoury choux, by adding cayenne pepper or paprika and omitting the castor sugar.

125 ml milk
100 g unsalted butter, diced
1 tspn castor sugar
4 eggs

125 ml water
½ tspn salt
150 g cake flour
eggwash, 1 egg yolk mixed with 1 T milk

Preheat oven to 180°C.
Combine the milk, water, butter, salt and sugar in a saucepan and set over low heat. Bring to the boil and immediately take the pan off the heat. Add the sifted flour and mix well with a wooden spoon until completely smooth. Return the paste to a medium heat and stir continuously for 1 minute to dry out the paste. Pour the paste into a bowl. Add the eggs, one at a time, beating well with the wooden spoon between each addition.

Once the eggs are all incorporated, the paste should be smooth and shiny with a thick ribbon consistency. Line a baking sheet with greaseproof paper. Put the choux paste into a piping bag fitted with a 1cm plain nozzle and pipe out 40 puffs, 3cm in diameter. Brush the choux with eggwash. Bake at 180°C for 15-20 minutes until the outside of the bun is dry and crisp but the inside is still soft. Cool on a wire rack. Fill with crème pâtissière.

Crème pâtissière au chocolat

6 egg yolks, large and free range
⅓ cup cake flour
100 g Lindt 70% Dark chocolate

⅔ cup castor sugar
2 cups full cream milk
Unsalted butter

Whisk the egg yolks and one third of the castor sugar together in a glass Pyrex bowl until pale yellow. Whisk in the flour thoroughly. In a saucepan, add the milk with the rest of the sugar and turn on the heat. Once the milk comes to the boil, pour it onto the egg mixture, stirring gently.

Pour the milk mixture back into the pan and gently bring to the boil stirring continuously with the whisk. Allow small bubbles to form on the surface of the custard for a couple of minutes. Melt the dark chocolate in a bain-marie and add to the custard. Pour the custard into a clean glass bowl and dot little pats of unsalted butter onto the custard surface to prevent a skin forming. Once the custard is cold, cover the bowl with cling film and refrigerate for up to 3 days until needed.

Oven roasted bananas

Serves 8

Bananas grow very easily on the South Coast. When we were children this dessert was a big hit. This easy and delicious dessert is served simply with a sprinkling of brown sugar. If you are entertaining then serve the oven roasted bananas with homemade avocado, coconut and vanilla bean ice-cream.

8 ripe bananas in their skins
Brown sugar for sprinkling

Preheat the oven to 190°C. Place the ripe bananas in their skins onto a flat ovenproof dish. Bake the bananas for 15 minutes until the skins start blistering. Remove from the oven. Place on dessert plates and serve with a light sprinkle of brown sugar or a scoop of the homemade ice-cream.

Nougat glacé with kiwi fruit coulis
Makes 8

Christmas in Mauritius is a special time of the year. Our Christmas menus do not conform to the Northern Hemisphere. Here in the Indian Ocean we make use of local produce and remain influenced by the hot tropical weather in December. This delicious ice-cream dessert was served at Bois Rouges, home of Tante Monique, first born of the five Moniques in our immediate family!

2 cups cream
40 g castor sugar
100 g almonds, ground
2 T Cointreau liqueur

5 egg whites
3 T honey
100 g glacé fruit, chopped

Macerate the chopped glacé fruit in the Cointreau. Line your loaf tin or terrine dish with cling wrap, ensuring sufficient overlap to cover the nougat glacé at the end. Boil the honey and castor sugar for 1 minute. Whip the egg whites until stiff and pour the hot honey in a thin stream onto the egg whites. Continue beating until the egg white has cooled down. In a separate bowl, whip the fresh cream until thick and unctuous. Fold the cream into the egg white mixture. Gently add the ground almonds and macerated glacé fruit. Pour the Nougat Glacé into the loaf tin and place in the freezer for at least 5 hours. Serve sliced with kiwi fruit coulis onto chilled dessert plates.

Kiwi Fruit Coulis
5 kiwis   50 g castor sugar

Peel the kiwis and cut them into four pieces. Remove the hard white core. Add the kiwi pieces and castor sugar to a liquidiser and purée until smooth. Use immediately. One can replace the ground almonds in the Nougat Glacé with chocolate nibs or dried raisins. In order for the Nougat Glacé to be well set and frozen it is preferable to use a metal mould. To serve, unmould the Nougat Glacé and using a long knife, dipped in hot water and wiped dry, slice the Nougat Glacé and place into chilled dessert plates. Pour the kiwi fruit coulis onto the sliced Nougat Glacé and serve.

Strawberry crumble with vanilla ice-cream

Makes 8

Strawberries in season have a heavenly smell. In KwaZulu-Natal we have a local supplier, Capenny Estates. Our favourite mountain biking spot is Holla Trails on the Collisheen Estate, near Ballito on the North Coast. If you're cycling some of the routes and you're fortunate enough to be with Trevor, he'll point out the strawberry fields and tunnels as well as all the beautiful bird species to be found at Holla. But beware, coming up there's also Mamba Alley where you'd better pedal for your life in case a black mamba is lurking in the bushes!

500 g strawberries, hulled and cut in 4
1 cup almond flour
½ cup Organic cold pressed virgin coconut oil
½ tspn cinnamon
Vanilla ice-cream to serve

Juice of 1 lemon
½ cup chopped macadamias
3 T honey
2 pinches sea salt

Preheat the oven to 190°C. Pop the strawberries in a dish and squeeze the juice of half the lemon over them. Toss lightly to coat the strawberries with the juice. Divide the strawberries amongst 8 ramekins. In a separate mixing bowl, combine the almond flour, macadamia nuts, coconut oil, remaining lemon juice, honey, cinnamon and salt. Mix gently. Spread the nut topping evenly over the strawberries and bake until the fruit is bubbly and the topping is golden brown (approximately 20 minutes). Serve with a quenelle of double thick cream. Serve with a scoop of vanilla ice-cream.

Index of recipes

Alphabetical index of recipes

Made in the USA
Lexington, KY
21 November 2017